Operation Iron Curtain

Retribution

відплата

Robert Dobbs

DEDICATION

A salute to the unyielding and unconquerable spirit of the human race, which, despite suffering, manages to keep going, make it through, and come out on top. This narrative is a monument to individuals who confront their concerns and choose to act, to those who aspire for a better world even though the way to get there is plagued with problems, and to those who are willing to act in spite of those hurdles.

Your sacrifices, which are most of the time unnoticed and unheard, are a demonstration of how strong human willpower can be. This is addressed to the men and women serving on the front lines of armed war. Those who hear your stories are inspired by your bravery and devotion, and they are reminded of the real price that must be paid for peace.

And last but not least, I would want to address you, the reader, who has chosen to participate in this adventure and to live vicariously through the lives of people who are only mirrors of our own challenges and successes. The fact that you are ready to sympathize, comprehend, and develop as a person is what makes these experiences worthwhile to share.

I raise a glass to the visionaries, the doers, and the unsung heroes that reside within each of us. You are the reason this book was written.

CONTENTS

"In the midst of chaos, there is also opportunity."

Sun Tzu, The Art of War

ACKNOWLEDGMENTS

Writing a book is almost never an individual activity, and this one is hardly an exception to that rule. There are many people who have helped to the production of this tale in a variety of ways, ranging from major to little, and I would want to use this opportunity to express my appreciation to each and every one of them.

To begin, I would want to express my gratitude to both my literary agency and my editor, whose comments and suggestions were extremely helpful in developing the narrative. Not only has your direction assisted in bringing this narrative to life, but it has also improved the quality of my writing.

During the part of the study where I was gathering information, various historians, military specialists, and conflict analysts were kind enough to share their time and expertise with me. I owe them a tremendous amount of gratitude. Because of your in-depth knowledge and experience in the subject matter, the depiction of the battle, its tactics, and the many facets of combat were accurate and convincing.

My immediate family as well as my close friends deserve special recognition since they have maintained an incredible amount of composure and support during this entire process. Your trust in me, even when I doubted myself, kept me going.

To conclude, I would want to say the following to all of the readers who have been there for me during this journey: Your energy, your comments, and your willingness to participate in the narrative have been genuinely motivating. I am writing this letter, above everything else, for you.

Many thanks to everyone.

INTRODUCTION

Every battle, conflict, or struggle has its own distinct narrative, which is a story that is fashioned from the strands of ambition, power, desperation, and, ultimately, the human spirit. This book intends to investigate one such tale, not to glorify battle but to highlight the power of the human spirit that may emerge from the ashes of conflict. The book's subtitle is "The Strength of the Human Spirit Can Emerge from the Ashes of Conflict." The narrative is an intersection of numerous points of view, including the political maneuverings of nations, the strategic calculations of generals, the unyielding endurance of troops, the determination of ordinary citizens caught up in exceptional situations, and so on. The reality that there is always a human tale at the center of every dispute is demonstrated by this fact.

Although the majority of this narrative is a work of fiction, it does incorporate aspects of real-world occurrences and the geopolitical dynamics of the modern day. It focuses on Ukraine, Russia, and Belarus, as well as the delicate dance of power that these three states participate in, and draws inspiration from the tension that exists in Eastern Europe at the present time. This book imagines a scenario in which these tensions rise into an open conflict, and in doing so, it shows the tremendous repercussions of war - not just on the battlefield, but also on the lives of individuals, their identities, and the overall trajectory of history.

The telling of this narrative allows us to be witnesses to the valor shown by men and women fighting on the front lines, the suffering encountered by people living in a landscape ravaged by war, the moral conundrums confronted by political leaders, and the intricate strategic considerations involved in contemporary combat. It highlights the possible costs of violence as well as the significance of peace, negotiation, and the peaceful resolution of disputes via diplomatic means.

This is not merely a narrative about war; rather, it is a story about the unbreakable spirit of mankind and how it can shine through even the darkest of times. It is a story of valor and selflessness, of choices taken under pressure in the heat of combat, and of the far-reaching effects those decisions have. It is a story as old as mankind itself, one of surviving against the odds and holding on to the unwavering belief that things would get better in the future.

We would like to take this opportunity to welcome you to a narrative that is both a gloomy reflection on the current state of affairs and a warning tale about the not-too-distant future. We would like to welcome you to the more human side of conflict.

CHAPTER 1 "THE UNSEEN SHADOWS"

The blackness of the night was slowly being pushed away by the first glimmer of morning, and the wide expanse of the border between Russia and Ukraine pulsed with an unsettling silence. War's churning machinery was starting to spin, but it was hidden by the misleading shroud of calm that had been cast over the situation. on the eerie stillness of the early morning, innumerable tracks were left on the snow-covered ground as an army began to discreetly collect under the shelter of the surrounding woodlands. In the next hours, the army would continue to gather in secrecy.

The skeleton silhouette of armored vehicles sat like gigantic predators just beyond the edge of the tree line. The gunmetal grey surfaces of the vehicles blended in well with the monochromatic winter environment. Nearby, troops could be seen congregating around fires that had been set in a hurry. Despite the fact that their breath was misting in the chilly air, their features remained stony and expressionless beneath the intense glare of portable lights. The echoes of loud directives, the clatter of feet against frozen soil, and the sporadic hum of motors; all of these things pointed to a gloomy preparation that bore an unsettling promise of the bloodshed that was to come.

A man emerged from the shadows and moved towards the middle of the activity that was being carried out by the soldiers. It was General Igor Sokolov, a man whose name reverberated throughout the ranks of the Russian army and instilled both dread and respect in those who heard it. His eyes were steely and perceptive as he gazed over the growing activity with a cunning glare. He was a behemoth of a guy, his huge shoulders clothed in a worn military coat. The Russian armed forces were morphing into an unbeatable war machine under his direction the entire time he was in charge of them. His reputation precedes him as a cunning tactician who was recognized as much for his unmatched ruthlessness as for his outstanding strategic acumen. His reputation preceded him.

Field Commander Andriy Petrovich was aware of the growing danger on the Ukrainian side of the border, where he was stationed at a basic command post in the capital city of Kyiv. He was a slender figure with sharp, hawkish features, and his grey hair was a testament to the many years he had spent on the battlefield. He stood in stark contrast to Sokolov. He was an unbreakable force, a soldier in every sense of the word, and he bravely bore the responsibility of his nation's liberation on his strong shoulders. Petrovich had little question about what was going to happen because Russia's activities were becoming more openly aggressive.

CIA analyst Elizabeth Palmer was completely immersed in the frenetic symphony of international intelligence while she was working in the middle of Washington, D.C., halfway across the world, an ocean away, and intimately tied to the battle that was building. Palmer was little in stature, with short, wavy hair that framed a face that was characterized by resolve and intelligence. Her perceptive observations had been instrumental in guiding the United States' foreign policy on more occasions than anybody would openly recognize.

During the time that Palmer was sorting through the papers that were piling up on her desk, her keen eyes picked up on the growing evidence of the Russian military buildup. In spite of protestations from the Kremlin, the pattern was obvious, as glaring as the chill that was beginning to settle into the bones of the people who were standing watch around Ukraine's borders.

Maxim Yurevich was getting ready for his own battle at the same time, but he was hiding out in some back alleyways of Minsk, Belarus, where no one was looking. Yurevich was a stout figure who had shaggy brown hair and deep-set eyes that glowed with an unquenchable fire. He was a freedom warrior who fought against the devotion that his own government had towards Russia. Because he had witnessed the tyrannical nature of Russian influence personally, he was in a unique position to comprehend the severe peril that Ukraine was facing. It's possible that his nation was forced into surrender, but he wasn't going to stand by and let Ukraine suffer the same fate without putting up a fight.

As Russia persisted in its unrelenting buildup of its military, the rest of the world watched and waited with bated breath for the spark that would set the dry tinder of international affairs ablaze. The strain was apparent, as it swept across borders, engulfed nations, put relationships to the test, and pushed the world closer and closer to an abyss of uncertainty.

Sokolov, Petrovich, Palmer, and Yurevich were all caught up in the currents of history as they worked their way through the oppressive atmosphere. Unbeknownst to them, their paths, which were formed by national allegiances, personal motives, and a shared sense of duty, would eventually converge, bringing them deep into the heart of a struggle that would test the resolve of both nations and individuals alike. Their adventure had hardly just started.

The globe was being drawn into a chaotic dance of power, survival, and resistance by the extending of the war's shadows, which were unseen. The performers were prepared to begin the first act of a frightening drama that was about to be enacted, and the stage was ready.

General Sokolov conducted his inspection of the troops while covered up in his military coat in the icy conditions that were prevalent at the border. His entire body, down to the smallest muscle and tendon, was acutely aware of the hum of impending confrontation that was permeating the atmosphere. He could see the features of his troops becoming jaded as a result of the severe cold, and in their eyes, he saw the same resolute resolve that was reflected in his own. The roar of the Russian bear could be heard ringing over the desolate, snow-covered terrain as it began to stir.

On the screen of the command center, which was hidden away in a somewhat unremarkable part of Kyiv, maps brimming with areas of possible criminal activity were displayed. A worn hand was following the curve of the Dnieper River when Commander Petrovich became vividly aware of the wolf at the door. His attention was fixated on the seemingly little red dots that indicated possible hostile movement. Each blip, each little pulse, indicated that the storm was becoming worse. He clinched his jaw, and each wave of anxiety etched deeper lines into his battle-hardened face. He was a man who had seen a lot of action.

Elizabeth Palmer struggled to unravel the mystery of Russian motivation while working at the CIA's headquarters, which were located on the other side of the wide Atlantic Ocean. Each newly obtained piece of intelligence, each satellite image, and each conversation that was intercepted represented another piece in the complex chess game that was being played out on the international arena. Her mind was on fire, with the embers of knowledge lighting the tinder of facts to create a raging inferno of comprehension in her head. The staccato rhythm that was being played by her fingers on the piano merged with the thumping that was being produced by her pounding heartbeat.

In the hidden safehouse that Maxim Yurevich kept in Minsk, he was obscured by the darkness, and the only thing that highlighted his form was the faint blue glow that emanated from the primitive communication gadget that he used. The darkly lighted room was filled with the sounds of whispered conversations, the crinkling of maps, and the rustling of notes that had been used for a long time. He was engaging in risky behavior and was just one misstep away from falling prey to the merciless teeth of his adversary. However, he was bolstered in his determination by the freedom-loving spirit that coursed through his blood.

A new day began despite the mounting anxiety that had been building up. The sun, which was a pale disc in the winter sky, produced long shadows that trembled across the terrain, giving the impression that it was almost anxious about the human drama that was taking on below.

General Sokolov, whose breath was misting as a result of the chilly weather, examined the power of the Russian army while maintaining a malicious smirk at the corner of his lips.

Petrovich, whose figure was carved against the backdrop of the sunrise in Kyiv, swore an oath of solemnity in which he vowed to protect his homeland until the very moment he breathed his last.

As Palmer's bleary eyes scanned the day's last reports, she began to feel the beginnings of a chilling dread as the pieces of the puzzle started to come together.

And Yurevich, who was encircled by his fellow revolutionaries at the moment, vowed to fight against the approaching storm, his voice bearing the ageless echo of David bravely standing against Goliath.

As the day came to a close, the precursor to war carried on, with each occurrence creating a ripple in the stormy sea that is geopolitics. The invisible shadows of war seemed to grow longer with each passing instant, extending out like cold fingers in an attempt to enfold the entire planet in their chilly grip.

In the icy interior of Russia, the landscape teemed with an ever-increasing force made of iron and steel. An ever-increasing number of battle tanks, armored personnel carriers, missile launchers, and mobile artillery were being amassed. Their presence was like a terrible ballet, with movements choreographed with fatal perfection; they were like an orchestra of power and dread conducted by General Sokolov. A symphony of oncoming battle could be heard wafting through the air, comprised of the deep rumbling of heavy equipment, the clang of metal, and the hoarse yells of commands.

Back in Kyiv, Andriy Petrovich was rounding up his forces and getting ready to tackle the problem head-on. Under his careful eye, Ukrainian soldiers conducted drills, their bodies moving with grim purpose and their faces, albeit youthful, carved with a determination that was beyond their years. The whirring of jet engines flying overhead, the rapid-fire chatter of automatic weapons, and the steady thud of boots striking the ground were the heartbeat of a nation getting ready for combat.

At this point, Elizabeth Palmer was completely involved in the assignment that she was working on at her workstation in Washington. Her fingers were laboriously moving over the keyboard, and each keystroke was an echo in the silence of the late hours. Images from satellites, numbers, and locations – each and every piece of information simply served to confirm her darkest suspicions. As she triggered an alarm, her heart hammered in her chest. She knew the urgency of her message would cut through the layers of red tape that stood in the way of its delivery.

Maxim Yurevich and his comrades maintained their covert operations when they were based in Minsk. As plots were devised, targets were singled out, and escape routes were plotted, the cramped room hummed with an intense level of activity. Maxim would occasionally take a glimpse at a little image that had a lot of wear and tear on it. This snapshot served as a continual reminder of what he was fighting for. His daughter turned around and stared at him with eyes that shone as brightly as the stars. It was a terrible world that stood in the way of her having a peaceful future, and Maxim would do whatever in his power to prevent that from happening.

Sokolov was the only one in his command tent when we arrived back to the Russian encampment. The maps were laid out in front of him, and each one was covered in marks and notations that could only be understood by him. His eyes, which were focused intently on the details of each line and symbol, resembled two shards of ice. The sole sign of the gratification that he gained from his well set out ideas was a gradual upward curl that formed on his upper lip.

When they got back to Kyiv, Petrovich discovered that he was by himself as well. During the deepest part of the night, the command center was an impenetrable bastion of stillness. He stood at the window, his gaze wandering as he stared out at the city as his companions slept inside the room. They were unaware of the storm that was approaching them, but their lights continued to shine brightly in the night.

Palmer pressed the "send" button on her report before leaving Washington. She released a breath that she hadn't been aware she was holding when the confirmation message appeared on the screen. The gravity of the situation pressed heavily on her, but the knowledge that she had done all she could to help gave her some solace.

Before placing the photograph of his daughter back into his pocket in Minsk, Yurevich gave it one more glance before doing so. A calm acceptance of the part he had been given flowed over him, bringing with it a sense of inner tranquility and composure. As soon as he went out into the night, his form vanished into the gloom, being consumed by the invisible shadows of the task he was assigned.

A terrifying sense of expectancy hovered over the planet as the intricate threads of this tale continued to weave, creating a mood that was equal parts dread and hope, twisted together in an intricate dance.

The sun rose over a globe that was on the verge of falling down a cliff as a new day began to dawn. In the frozen plains of Russia, General Sokolov gave an address to his men, and the reverberations of his baritone voice could be heard through the quiet air. Every single soldier listened to him speak with rapt attention as the spoke of honor, duty, and homeland. Their hearts were thumping with a strong mix of anticipation and dread as they listened. The words were part of a recurring motif, but in the presence of Sokolov's chilling gaze, they took on a sinister import.

Petrovich was doing the same thing in Ukraine at the time. He carried himself with an air of confidence and stoicism, his severe countenance serving as a symbol of the tenacity of the Ukrainian people. His comments produced a picture of their country, not just as a physical entity, but also as a living, breathing organism that flourished in the hearts of the people who lived there. He did not simply refer to it as a geographical entity. His gaze traversed the plethora of faces that were in front of him, each one being a representation of the unyielding willpower of the Ukrainian people.

A flurry of activity had been sparked as a result of Palmer's report while this was going on in Washington. The sacred corridors of the CIA were buzzing with activity as teams raced to verify the material and take appropriate action. She felt a sort of terrible satisfaction wash over her as she watched the pandemonium unfold before her eyes. She had completed her duties, and at this point it was up to the people in charge to carry out their responsibilities.

Maxim Yurevich was making his way through the shadier parts of Minsk at the time. While everyone in the city was asleep and oblivious to the political upheaval that was developing, he and his squad set off on their dangerous mission. Although each step was laden with peril, the men advanced with an unshakeable composure, the gravity of their mission evident in the expressions on their expressionless faces.

On the other side of the border with Russia, the tremendous war machine was now operating at full capacity. The air was thick with the rumble of motors and the buzz of electronics, creating an eerie symphony that spoke of battle and destruction. Sokolov, who was in charge of supervising the operation, experienced a gloomy sense of fulfillment. His plans were coming together nicely; very soon, people all across the world will be able to experience the power of the Russian bear.

After giving a speech to his men in Kyiv, Petrovich made his way back to the command post he was assigned to. He was prepared for what was to come. All of the warning signs, including the disorganized maps on his table, the flashing lights, and the muffled voices, pointed to the impending storm. As he readied himself for the test, he could see in his eyes a resolute determination that would not be shaken. They would struggle, but ultimately, they would prevail.

On the other side, Elizabeth Palmer found herself in the position of playing a waiting game. She listened in silence while her bosses discussed the matter, their expressions stern and their voices low. In spite of the heated debates, there was an unsettling calm that appeared to linger in the air. It was as if the whole world was holding its breath while waiting for what was inevitably going to happen.

And Maxim Yurevich, as he made his way through the darkly illuminated streets of Minsk, could feel the excitement of defiance racing through his veins. There was a glimmer of hope in his eyes, a raging need for independence that could not be extinguished by anything. As he vanished into the darkness, his spirit merged with the shadows that were moving about him but nobody could see them.

The globe was poised on the precipice of doom, and the atmosphere was filled with nervous energy, terror, as well as hope and resistance. The game of power, survival, and resistance continued to play out in a symphony of hidden shadows as each player made their move on this intricate chessboard.

During the time when the reverberations of Sokolov's speech were still lingering heavily in the air, the Russian war machine began to roar to life. The early silence was broken by the buzzing of drones and the sound of armored vehicles as the snow crunched underneath heavy tank treads. Each soldier, the moisture from their breath creating a mist in the icy air, took their position in this mammoth machine. They moved as one, a relentless flood of force, ready to burst forward at the signal of their commander. Their eyes were steely, and their hearts were firm.

Petrovich, who was in Kyiv at the time, looked at the screen and noticed that the number of red dots indicating enemy activity had increased. However, despite the fact that the adversary was alert and ravenous, Ukraine was not an easy kill. He observed as tanks and personnel from the Ukrainian army began to take their places, and he saw that the determination in their eyes mirrored his own. He was aware of the usual burden of leadership beginning to settle on his shoulders. This was his nation, and these were his people; he was damned if he was going to let them go without putting up a fight to defend themselves.

Palmer was meeting with the Director of the Central Intelligence Agency (CIA) over in Washington. The tension in the air could be felt throughout the room. Images captured by satellite were displayed on a wide screen, showing Russian forces massing in close proximity to the Ukrainian border. Every new image and every new click served as a jarring reminder of the coming catastrophe. Palmer experienced a sickening feeling in the pit of her stomach, but she managed to keep her calm throughout the ordeal. She could not afford to hedge her bets because the risks were so high.

Yurevich and his crew walked eerily through the darkly illuminated alleyways of Minsk as if they were wraiths. Their hearts seemed to be beating to a constant rhythm of adrenaline and anxiety, as if the stillness of the city were vibrating in their ears. Each action was executed with exactitude, and every step had been meticulously planned. They were the invisible specters in the darkness, and the stars in the sky and the cause that they battled for were the only ones who were aware of their existence.

Sokolov's soldiers, which were stationed on the outskirts of the Ukrainian border, presented an ominous profile against the bleak winter sky as the day progressed. The general looked out over the immensity of his army from the command truck he was riding in. His icy smile betrayed a smug air of contentment that was just visible around the edges. The results of his careful preparation were about to become apparent.

The situation was quite tense in the command center that Petrovich had established. Every passing minute pushed them that much closer to facing the unavoidable. Petrovich's calm manner and unwavering tone served as an anchor for his crew as the storm raged around them. He was like a lighthouse in the storm. His attention was unwaveringly focused on the displays, and the steady beat of the clock could be heard reverberating in his chest.

Palmer sat in the very center of the CIA headquarters and saw the process of formulating a response to her report. Words were traded, proposals were discussed, and conclusions were drawn. She had finished her work, and it was now up to the decision-makers to take the next step. She forced herself to ignore the gnawing sensation of powerlessness that she was experiencing. She was responsible for doing a task, and she intended to do it to the very best of her ability.

During this time, Maxim Yurevich and his companions had successfully completed their mission. As they got to work, there was an air of grim resolve among those who were participating. Every individual was aware of what was at risk, and they were all prepared to pay the price for it. They continued to work covertly as the noises of the city gradually came to life, their acts serving as a prelude to the resistance that was still to come.

As the sun began to set, the entire globe appeared to be poised on the precipice of a chasm. All of the players were in their proper positions, and the tension was building. All that was required was a push or a trigger to start the chain reaction of happenings that would alter the path that history would take.

Sokolov was standing at his command post, which was lighted by harsh fluorescent lights, and he was pondering the significance of the order that was about to be given to him. His index finger was hovering above a bright red button, which was the activation mechanism for the attack. His steely eyes swept over the collected maps and intelligence reports as his thoughts traced over each plan and counterplan he had painstakingly devised. Knowing that he had such an immense amount of power gave him a rush of excitement and adrenaline like nothing else could.

Petrovich and his counselors were back in Kyiv taking in the most recent satellite feed when it was brought to their attention. As he looked in the tremendous show of Russian soldiers at his border, the whites of his knuckles began to become white around the margins of the screen. He could feel the command center's walls pressing in on him, and the weight of the situation was sucking the oxygen out of the room. Even though his pulse was pounding in his chest, he kept a level head and the fire of determination burned stronger in his eyes.

Palmer walked impatiently throughout the CIA headquarters in Washington while the higher-ups discussed what action to do in reaction to the situation. The tension in the room was so thick that she could practically taste it. In the heated quiet, everything appeared to be exaggerated, from the faint hum of discussion to the ruffling of papers and the tapping on the computer. Despite the fact that her head was spinning with ideas and her stomach was in knots from nervousness, she clutched to her responsibility like a lifeline.

During this time, Yurevich and the others working with him were deep in the throes of their operation in the seedy underbelly of Minsk. As they huddled over plans, the eerie shadows generated by the faint light from a single bulb cast spooky shadows as they whispered in a ghostly mumble. In spite of the fact that the stakes were higher than they had ever been before and the risk was tangible, they moved with a precision that betrayed an unwavering determination.

As Sokolov eventually issued the order, the tension in the

command post where he was stationed was at an all-time high. As his men began their march, he watched with a predatory grin as the ground began to shake under the power of his war machine. It was a scene that had the potential to evoke feelings of both wonder and dread in its viewers. A sense of icy contentment began to permeate his entire being. The competition had at long last started.

As soon as the foreign invaders entered Ukrainian soil, the sirens in Petrovich's command center began to sound. The information displayed on the screens portrayed a bleak picture as Russian soldiers continued to advance, their numbers becoming overwhelming. The muscles in Petrovich's jaw contracted, and he tightened his hold on the command baton. He was hit by a surge of grim resolve and it swept over him. This was the end. The time for which they had been making preparations.

The news of the invasion rocked the intelligence establishment in Washington once it was revealed that it had occurred. Palmer stared helplessly as the mayhem exploded all around her, a sobering realization beginning to set in. Her report had not been excessively alarming; rather, it had been spotted on. Her pulse raced with a feeling that was equal parts vindication and fear as the implications began to become apparent.

The word of the invasion reached Yurevich and his troops as they were finishing up their mission. Their expressions became more resolute, and their resolve became more ironclad. Their mission had taken on a new significance, and time was of the essence. They were no longer merely opposing a dictatorship; at this point, they were against an invading force.

The world as we knew it will never be the same again once darkness fell. The terrifying specter of war had been let free, and its cry could be heard reverberating across continents. The competition had begun, and all of the players were engaged in a dangerous dance. The previously hidden shadows made their appearance at last, unveiling the entirety of their menacing shape in the process.

The night was illuminated by the flames of war, and the previously calm stretches were transformed into a cacophony by the booming cannons and screaming engines of the conflict. From his command position, Sokolov was able to observe his soldiers as they advanced into Ukraine like a well-oiled machine designed to dominate and cause havoc. His heart was beating at a furious pace in his chest, creating a macabre symphony of power and control that was in perfect harmony with the mayhem that was taking place in front of him.

Petrovich stood as a bastion of stability in the middle of the mayhem that prevailed in Kyiv. His attention was riveted on the displays, which displayed the fast advancement of Russian soldiers. He yelled out instructions, his voice acting as a rock of stability in the midst of the roaring tempest of conflict. His determination became a wall that could not be breached as a result of the tremendous and unyielding weight of authority. He would engage in combat. They would all do that. right up until the very end.

The situation room of the Central Intelligence Agency was a whirlwind of frenzied activity over in Washington. Palmer remained on the outside of the conflict as her report became a foreboding reality. The truth was a difficult pill to accept in that moment. The critical nature of the issue resounded throughout the room, and everyone's expression changed to one of severe anxiety. The weight of the circumstances was beginning to weigh heavily on Palmer's mind, and she had a growing sense of dread as a result.

Yurevich and his squad were in a race against time as they made their way through the hidden underworld of Minsk. The news of the invasion gave their activities a sense of increased immediacy that had previously been lacking. Each piece of intelligence, as well as each sabotage operation that had been planned, was now a potential lifeline in the next conflict. The grim resolve and hushed prayers of men who were willing to put everything on the line filled the concealed bunker, making the atmosphere within feel oppressive.

Sokolov was clearly a man possessed by something. His command center served as the operation's nerve core, where all of the plans and operations were meticulously planned to achieve maximum effectiveness. As instructions were being passed along, the anxiety was evident; the approaching troops were like an unrelenting tsunami that was slamming against the Ukrainian line.

In Kyiv, Petrovich responded to every maneuver with a counterattack, and his mind was a whirlwind of strategies and counterattacks. He gave orders to his soldiers, and the defense they provided was a solid barrier against the Russian attack. In the middle of the smoke and flames, he shone like a beacon of hope; despite the raging tempest, his soul remained unbroken.

During this time, Palmer was experiencing an empty feeling in her stomach as she watched the crisis escalate in Washington. She had the impression that she had no control over the nightmare that was her life. But she had a job to complete, and she stuck to it, her analytical mind working overtime to supply insight and knowledge that may tip the scales. She was determined to get the job done.

While Yurevich and his crew were finishing up their mission back in Minsk, their preparations served as a jarring reminder of the perilous road that lay ahead of them. Their fight was a little spark in the growing darkness, a monument to their unconquerable spirit and steadfast confidence in freedom. Their resistance was a small flame in the growing gloom.

The night continued on into the early hours of the morning, leaving a permanent mark on the globe in the form of a threat of war. The game had only just started, yet already the participants were caught up in a dangerous dance; the outcome of the game was shaping up to be a fascinating story of power, resistance, and survival.

Sokolov's soldiers continued to push deeper into Ukrainian territory as the first rays of light fought to make their way through the thick blanket of smog that covered the sky. The constant sound of artillery fire and the hum of airplanes flying overhead continued to play as the war's music in the background. Sokolov, who was deeply involved in the planning and execution of this mission, relished the rush of adrenaline that was going through his body. His desire for success, which had been a burning flame, had grown into a raging inferno that was devouring everything in its path.

Petrovich gathered his troops in the middle of Kyiv in order to defend the city from the unrelenting assault. His resolve became more resolute with each new defeat and every obstacle that he encountered. He was aware of the price that had to be paid for this battle, which was being paid in the form of tears and blood. Even though his heart hurt, he was steadfast in his determination. The Ukrainian people were a hardy and determined people; they would not submit without a spirited struggle.

Palmer, who was located on the other side of the world in Washington, was feeling an increasing sense of hopelessness as he watched the event unfold. It seemed as if the muted blues and reds of the map on the screen were making fun of her, with each blink representing a new level of ruin and loss. Her hands were balled up into fists at her sides, and her professional mask completely concealed the anguish that was going on inside of her. But she was not assaulted in any way. She was used to overcoming challenges, and she would continue to do so in the future.

Yurevich and his gang were racing against the ticking time as they made their way through the gloomy underworld of Minsk. Their modest uprising, which was only a covert symbol of resistance, was getting ready to shine its light. Their goal had evolved into a means of survival, a beacon of hope in the face of the bleak reality that was becoming. Yurevich, who was in charge, gritted his teeth and hardened his determination. They were unwavering in their commitment because they believed their cause to be right.

When we got back to the border, Sokolov's victory was a terrifying sight to behold. His armies pushed forward like an unstoppable wave, with each conquered city serving as evidence of their superior strength. His command center was abuzz with news of victories, which fed his voracious ambition to establish dominance. He was on the verge of creating history, and he was not going to let anything or anybody get in his way.

The situation was dire, but not entirely hopeless, according to the command center run by Petrovich. The Ukrainian resistance became more resolute with each subsequent Russian assault. The voice of Petrovich reverberated throughout the room, serving as a call to arms amidst the mayhem. His trust in his people was unshakeable; he had no doubt that they would weather the storm and emerge victorious.

Palmer put in an incredible amount of work in Washington. Each and every piece of intelligence and report was inspected and evaluated in great detail. Her part in the ongoing crises on a worldwide scale has never been more important. She was the link between knowledge and action, and her mind was working at a breakneck pace to piece together the pieces of the murderous dance that was taking place across the ocean.

During this time, Yurevich and his squad began their operation, which was a brave demonstration of resistance against the Russian soldiers that were advancing. Their resoluteness shined stronger as daylight broke, throwing long shadows against the horrible current of the fight. They were the invisible heroes, and the beacon of hope amid the looming gloom was the courage that they displayed.

The entire globe was on the edge of its seat as the first day of the battle came to a conclusion. The threat of armed confrontation loomed large; its menacing profile carved against the blood-spattered morning sky. This was simply the beginning, the opening act of a story about surviving against the odds and showing no fear. And when the day rose, it cast light on a world that had been changed irrevocably, a world that was precariously balanced on the brink of the abyss.

Sokolov commanded his soldiers throughout the day with the skill of a grandmaster moving chess pieces. The day stretched on. He found that the hammering beat of combat was like music to his macabre ears, and that the destruction was a tribute to his strength. His eyes, which shone with a steely gleam of resolve, rarely wandered away from the ever-changing battlefield maps. Each city in Ukraine that was marked with a red dot was a triumphant symphony, and each kilometer that he traveled brought him one step closer to his ideal future.

In Kyiv, Petrovich displayed the dogged determination of a

grizzled veteran fighter as he bore the responsibility of defense and revenge. His resolve hardened like steel that had been tempered in the highest fire with each new report that detailed the advancement of the invading force. His commands reverberated throughout his command center, which was like a beating heart in the middle of the violent storm. He was the shining example of hope for his oppressed nation, and his people could not afford for him to fail them.

Palmer was a man who moved quickly and efficiently around the CIA's offices and hallways. Every tidbit of information that she obtained and every report that she perused became another weapon in her armory. Her desk was her stronghold, a barricade against the onslaught of knowledge that was coming her way. Her mind was working frantically to put together the massive jigsaw puzzle that is this mounting catastrophe, and her eyes, which were tired but determined, examined the most recent satellite feeds and army movement charts.

Yurevich and his rebels were the hidden undercurrent that was struggling against the flood underneath the busy streets of Minsk. Their subdued uprising, which was a glimmer of defiance among the tidal wave of repression, gained steam with each passing hour. Their resolve only became more resolute when word of the Russian advances made its way to them. They were no longer simply opposing a dictatorship; rather, they were engaged in a military conflict.

Sokolov took great pleasure in the melody of his master plan as he stood on the boundary. Both the canvas and the soundtrack of his victory were provided by the smoke-filled sky and the melancholy symphony of artillery fire. His heart raced in a frantic, almost animalistic pace of exhilaration with each new piece of information that was brought to his attention. He was making history and molding the world into his own image while he did it.

Back in Kyiv, Petrovich responded to each new development with an unyielding determination. His intellect was scorched with the pain of the injured and the dispossessed, and his heart reverberated with a melancholy song for those who had been lost. But despite this, his soul, which was unconquerable and obstinate, responded favorably to the call to arms. His determination, which was driven by his love for his country and its people, served as both his shield and his weapon.

Palmer, who was in Washington, struggled to come to terms with the seriousness of the developing events. Her heart was pounding in her chest as she struggled to come to terms with the gravity of the situation. In spite of everything, her intellect, which was like a stronghold in the midst of the storm, analyzed every bit of data and every piece of knowledge. Her alertness served as an uninterrupted line of defense in the conflict that was taking place thousands of miles away, and she was a sentinel.

Yurevich and the other members of his group planned their next action while they were in Minsk. Their activity, which was a shining example of defiance against the prevailing evil, gained ground. They were more determined than ever after hearing the news from the front lines, and their purpose is now an essential vein in the body of the resistance.

As darkness fell on the first day of the conflict, the entire globe held its breath in anticipation. The shadows, which were before undetectable, now made a lengthy and ominous silhouette against the blood-red sky. This was just the beginning of a story about surviving against the odds and showing resistance, a story that would determine the fate of entire nations as well as the future of the entire planet.

As the sun began to set on the first day of the conflict, it appeared as though the entire planet stopped breathing. The previously beautiful vistas were now marred by the charred wounds left by the fighting. But despite everything that was going on, mankind managed to keep going.

Sokolov, stationed in his command center, observed the day's conclusion with a victorious sense of accomplishment. He was well aware of the raw power that his position bestowed upon him as well as the sheer extent of his impact. His soldiers were the fangs of the beast of war, tearing and gnawing their way through the fabric of a once tranquil land with every step they took. The darkness descended upon him like a shroud, its depths concealing the aspirations he harbored inside them.

Petrovich viewed the city of Kyiv from the command center he was stationed in. The city's customary vitality had been replaced with the anxious expectation of a citizenry that was under attack. He was filled with a heady mixture of dread and resolve, and it was making his heart hurt. The night was drawing closer, yet the approaching darkness did not have the power to dampen their spirits. They would maintain their steadfastness, serving as a bulwark against the impending storm.

Palmer's eyes were glued to the displays as he watched them from Washington, which is located across the Atlantic. Her expression reflected the worsening predicament, yet her will shone through like a beacon of light against the growing darkness. She was one of the keepers of the delicate balance that had to be maintained since the planet was precariously poised on the edge of a knife. The storm that was raging inside was a sharp reflection of the darkness that was outside.

Yurevich brought his gang together deep within the maze-like tunnels under Minsk. Their expressions, which could only be made out by the dim glow of the bunker's lights, were those of unwavering determination. The battle had barely started, and all that stood between them and victory was a glimmer of light in the encroaching gloom. They were the hidden heroes, the peaceful people who resisted in secret. Their determination appeared even more clearly as the night progressed.

The participants in this dangerous game finally had a chance to stop and collect their breath as the day came to a close. Under the moonless night sky, their thoughts, which were entwined with both dread and determination, reverberated. The echo resonated, serving as a terrifying reminder of the fight in which they were currently engaged, a war that was not even close to being done.

The day for these distinct yet in some way interconnected characters had come to an end, but their narratives and their conflicts were only getting started. They were now a part of a broader story that had still to be told, a story about survival and defiance that was still in the works. Even though it was dark out, there was a lot of noise throughout the night. The reverberations of the fight from earlier hung heavily in the air, serving as a foreshadowing of the difficulties that were to come with the arrival of the new day.

CHAPTER 2 "RECOGNITION AND REBELLION"

The news that came from Moscow caused waves to be felt all around the world, much like a pebble being thrown into a lake. A courageous move, the recognition of the Donetsk People's Republic (DPR) and the Luhansk People's Republic (LPR) posed a challenge to the rest of the world. It was a rumbling introduction to the oncoming deluge that was still some time away.

Sokolov smiled sarcastically as he watched the program from his command center while he was listening to it. The announcement was a brilliant move, a strategic triumph that sent the rest of the globe reeling in confusion. Sokolov experienced an overwhelming sense of fulfillment as he saw the red banners of the DPR and LPR being raised in the Kremlin. His way was made clear, and everything was ready for him to provide a fantastic performance.

The news sent shockwaves across Kyiv when it was announced. Petrovich was beginning to feel the crushing burden of the weight of the announcement descend on his shoulders, and it was threatening to bring him to his knees. His guys turned at him with expressions that combined fear and defiance on their faces. He noticed that they were afraid, but more than that, he noticed that they were determined. They were his countrymen and his brothers in arms, and he could depend on them to fight to the death before submitting.

Palmer, who was located on the other side of the ocean in Washington, followed the events surrounding the Russian statement with a combination of skepticism and grim conviction. Even though she had been paying attention to the clues and the repositioning of the pieces on the geopolitical chessboard, the boldness of the play nevertheless left her in a state of disbelief. She did not appear to be paying attention as she sat back in her chair, her sight wandering and her mind racing. This was a flagrant escalation, a provocation that could not be ignored, and it caused the situation to become more dangerous.

The story quickly made its way through Yurevich's ranks in Minsk and spread like wildfire. There was a quiet hum of outrage and determination emanating from their underground bunker. There was a buzzing of whispers. A clear challenge and a smack in the face to their fight, the recognition of the separatist republics by Russia was a direct challenge. Yurevich had a blazing wave of rage, but he was able to stifle it almost instantly. It was not the moment for irrational outbursts of emotion; rather, it was the time for premeditated acts of defiance.

While the news reverberated through the halls of power and the gloomy trenches of the battlefield, every participant in this lethal game prepared for the next act. They braced themselves for the storm that was approaching, their hearts hammering with a mix of terror, rage, and resolve as they prepared for it.

Petrovich gathered his men in the middle of Kyiv for the rallying cry. His voice, which had become raspy from the exertion of the day, resounded throughout the command center, reaching each and every person who was under his authority. His comments were like a lighthouse, a rallying cry that gave them the strength and determination to carry out their mission. Petrovich had a flood of emotion as he spoke about their birthplace and the hardship that they faced together while he was speaking. They would fight to the death to protect their homeland and their people, which they considered to be sacred.

Sokolov experienced a tingling sensation of anticipation as he watched the transmission from his command center. His soldiers were prepared, and the mechanisms of war were all set up and waiting to be activated. As the red flags flapped in the Moscow sky, he turned to his command center with a predatory gleam in his eyes and a sense of delight. He was prepared to produce a performance that would be engraved into the annals of history, and he was aware that the whole world was watching.

In Washington, Palmer started putting together the pieces of the puzzle. The Russian announcement caused a seismic upheaval in the global scene, and the implications will have a significant impact in the future. While she was going over the information, her thoughts were racing with many possibilities. She served as the essential link between the gathering of intelligence and the implementation of that intelligence. The rules were now different, and she needed to adjust to them as rapidly as possible.

In Minsk, Yurevich and his countrymen girded themselves for the fight ahead. The fact that Russia acknowledged the independence of the separatist republics served as a jarring reminder of their purpose and reaffirmed their commitment to the fight. They were the hidden heroes and the voices that were never heard. Their determination became more resolute as rumors of a mutiny spread. They were a little spark, but they would light a fire of resistance if they were allowed to continue.

In the hours that followed, there was a frenetic tornado of preparation and planning to be done. The tension was tangible, a live wire of expectancy that sped through the center of each operation, from the glistening corridors of power in Moscow and Washington to the grimy frontlines in Ukraine and the hidden networks in Minsk. The stress was palpable, a live wire of anticipation that zipped through the heart of each operation.

Sokolov took great pleasure in the tense situation, which he oversaw from his command center. The flurry of activity, the frantic reports and commands that were being sent via the air, and everything else that was happening were all components of the big symphony that he was leading. His eyes, icy and analytical, swept over the deployment charts while his mind, which was already one step ahead, plotted the initial strike. He was a kingpin getting ready for the pursuit, like a hunter getting ready for the hunt. He was seeing his dominoes fall into place.

On the other hand, Petrovich was a stronghold in the midst of the storm. There was a flurry of activity in the central parts of the city of Kyiv. Everyone, from little children to elderly adults, shared a common goal: to protect their city and their place of residence. Petrovich exemplified the spirit of resiliency as he organized the defenses, recruited his soldiers, and hardened their positions. He served as a guiding light for his people as they navigated the impending storm.

Palmer's workstation was an oasis of peace in the midst of a sea of disorder on the other side of the ocean. She started putting together the pieces of the enemy's scheme as intelligence reports and satellite photographs began to pour in. Her brain, which had been trained over the course of many years of experience, was able to make connections, draw similarities, and predict moves. She was racing against the clock to give her country the advantage it needed, so she unraveled the information thread by thread as the clock ticked.

Yurevich's group served as a symbol of defiance deep within the heart of the busy metropolis of Minsk. They were diligently working every minute that went by, gathering intelligence, planning attacks, and mobilizing support. They were a raging fire in the midst of the raging storm that was the silent uprising. As word spread that Russia had acknowledged them, the importance of their mission increased significantly. They weren't simply fighting for Belarus; they were battling for the fundamental core of what it is to be free.

The stage had been prepared. The characters, each of whom were living in their own universe, stood on the precipice, ready to take the plunge into the void. Each passing second was a stride closer to the inevitable confrontation, a trek deeper into the eye of the storm.

Sokolov was in Moscow when he lifted his glass to the enormous screen that was portraying the flapping flags of both the DPR and the LPR. As a hunter salivating at the thought of the pursuit, the eagerness in his eyes betrayed how much he was looking forward to it. As he made his move, the world watched, unaware of the magnificent show that was going to take place in the very next moment.

Petrovich assembled his commanders in Kyiv, all of whom had grim but determined expressions on their faces. He couldn't help but feel a surge of pride as they deliberated about tactics and assessed the state of their assets. They were the underdogs, but that did not mean they were going to give up without a fight. Even though the odds were stacked against them, they possessed something that their adversary did not: the will of a unified people.

Palmer, who was in Washington, ran her fingers over the satellite photographs as her forehead was wrinkled in intense concentration. This was not merely a game of chess; rather, it was a conundrum, a maze of alternatives through which she had to find her way. As she pieced together the missing pieces, she experienced a rush of exhilaration. This was her battleground, and she was prepared to engage in the conflict.

Yurevich and his colleagues spent time in Minsk preparing for their part in the unfolding of this global drama. They were the unseen participants, yet their activities could be heard reverberating in the background. The suspense was palpable throughout the bunker as they worked to put the finishing touches on their preparations. They were prepared to launch an assault, further fanning the flames of insurrection.

The globe seemed to stop moving and stared into the darkness as if trying to catch its breath before dawn. The bustle that had prevailed before had subsided, and now there was a time of silence, a silence that seemed to envelop everything in an eerie stillness. The great play was about to begin, and everything was ready to go on stage, including the performers and the curtain.

Sokolov was in Moscow when morning broke, and the rays of light reflected in his icy, analytical eyes. The day had finally arrived, a day that would go down in history. He had carefully considered his course of action and carefully weighed each of his actions and decisions. The time for preparation had passed, and now it was time to put those plans into action.

Petrovich stood in Kyiv and looked over the city as the first rays of dawn lit up the faces of the men under his command. Each and every one of them was ready to give his life for his community, for the country he called home. Petrovich was aware of the magnitude of the burden that rested on his shoulders and weighed heavily on him. Turning away from the window, he fixed his eyes on the map spread out on the table. On it were lines and marks representing lives, families, and possible futures. He girded his loins and prepared himself for what was to come.

Palmer was in Washington reading through the latest reports when we met her. Her fingers flew across the keyboard and her mind raced. She had stayed up all night sifting through the data, analyzing each piece of information and gathering as much information as she could. She leaned back in her chair and stared intently at the bright screen as the first rays of morning sunlight filtered into her office. This was the end. The time had come for accountability.

Yurevich and the other members of his team sat close together in Minsk, the warm glow of their computer screens illuminating their faces. They were prepared for the worst-case scenario, but they hoped for the best possible outcome. Every single one of them was aware of the dangers and possible costs of their uprising. Nevertheless, they were ready to make a sacrifice for their independence and their country. Yurevich felt a terrible determination come over him as the first light of morning penetrated their bunker. They were ready to go into battle.

As the darkness was gradually dispelled by the dawn's first rays, the actual magnitude of the upcoming battle started to become more apparent.

In the center of Moscow, the city was just starting to wake up to the rhythm of normal life, completely ignorant to the drama that was about to unfold. While safely ensconced in his command center, Sokolov awaited the completion of the reports that had been compiled by his superiors. His men were prepared, their locations had been secured, and they had rehearsed their schemes down to the tiniest detail. As he issued the command for the advance, he had a tingling sensation of anticipation that ran down his spine. It was time to start moving the pieces about on the massive chessboard that represented the conflict.

In Kyiv, the city itself was like a fortification getting ready for an assault. The discouraging news that the Russians were making progress was sent to the steadfast commander, Petrovich. His pulse was pounding violently in his chest, but he remained unflinching in his determination. He rallied his men, and the sound of his voice reverberated throughout the city. "This is our home, and we will not let them take it from us without a fight." His comments, which were powerful and unyielding, lifted the spirits of his men and women and ignited a flame of resolve in the hearts of all of them.

Palmer was a flurry of focused activity while being located on the other side of the world in the quiet halls of the CIA. From the rush of reports that were flooding in, she was able to put together the developing scenario. As she tried to anticipate the next step taken by the adversary, her thoughts raced like a top. The stakes were enormous, and each new piece of information had the potential to completely alter the course of events. She held her tone calm as she reported her findings to the highest echelons of power, knowing full well that her observations had the potential to swing the outcome in their favor.

The gang of rebels led by Yurevich was a whirlwind of organized disorder that was hiding underneath the busy streets of Minsk. The bunker they were in became an increasingly tense environment as word of the Russian approach made its way down. Their part in the drama that was taking on had taken on new significance as a result. They weren't simply fighting for their own liberation; they were also fighting for the freedom of their brothers and sisters who lived in Ukraine. As they began carrying out their plans, their actions were quick and precise since they were all well aware that the slightest error may result in significant losses for them.

The entire globe was captivated as each new development in the drama caused a chain reaction of responses across the international stage. The initial movements had been made, and the introductory act had come to an end. The board was prepared, and play had already begun with all of the pieces. It was time to get down to business and start playing the actual game.

The tension grew steadily worse during the course of the day. The announcement that Russia had recognized the DPR and LPR sent shockwaves across the globe, upsetting the delicate balance of power and igniting a frenzy all over the world. The future of Ukraine hung in the balance as governments tried to find a solution, news channels broadcasted constant updates, and the world watched.

Our protagonists were caught up in their own personal issues right in the middle of the drama that was unfolding. Every single one of them had to overcome their own internal demons in addition to the obstacles that came from the outside world.

Sokolov struggled to come to terms with the gravity of his decision when he was in Moscow. The initial excitement of the approach was quickly replaced by the somber realization of the impending fight. The consequences of his decisions became increasingly apparent to him as each hour passed. Despite this, he never wavered in his resolve; he was a rock of unwavering tenacity. Every choice he made and every command he issued started a domino effect that spread across the ranks and influenced how the battle unfolded.

Petrovich discovered that he was forced to walk a tightrope in Kyiv. On one side, there was the disheartening truth of the invasion, and on the other, there were the hopeful faces of his warriors, whose determination was steadfast in spite of the odds. His direction was a light in the darkness for them, and they clung to every word he spoke and every order he issued like it was a lifeline.

At the national capital, Palmer struggled to keep up with the quickly advancing intelligence. Her thoughts were a maelstrom of potential outcomes and scenarios, and her mind was a battleground of different plans and counterstrategies. Palmer found herself in the middle of the storm as the consequences of Russia's recognition became clear to the rest of the globe. Her observations were the key to interpreting the strategies employed by the adversary.

While in Minsk, Yurevich and his crew operated covertly, keeping the outside world in the dark about their whereabouts and activities. The consequences of failure were severe, and they ran the risk of losing their lives at any moment. In spite of the risks, they carried out their goal with unyielding determination, the struggle for freedom serving as the driving force behind all they did.

As the story progressed, every character was challenged to the point of their breaking point. They had to overcome obstacles that put their mettle to the test, deal with choices that would define their destinies, and struggle with the implications of the decisions they made. And as everyone across the world waited with bated breath, the scene was being prepared for the next act of this international play.

A state of global upheaval had been brought about. The escalating crisis prompted responses from governments all around the world, each of which was attempting to negotiate its way through the complex web of international politics and alliances. The leaders were put in a position where they had to make tough choices, each of which had the potential to tilt the balances in favor of one side or the other. The entire globe was a ticking time bomb waiting to go off at any moment.

Sokolov's day in Moscow had been like riding an adrenaline-fueled roller coaster ride all the way through. His years of diligent preparation were put to the test as his precise preparations were finally put into effect. He observed as his warriors moved, their motions becoming increasingly powerful and precise as they went. Sokolov took some time to think as the sun set over the city and darkness fell. The game had just started, and he had taken the initiative by making the first move. However, he was not naive in any way. The path that lay before was littered with obstacles, and the outcomes of each given choice may determine whether or not success was achieved.

The day presented a challenge to Petrovich's authority in Kyiv. The city had been shaken up by the news of the Russian assault, but Petrovich was able to keep the morale of his troops high throughout the ordeal. His thoughtful preparation and passionate remarks had maintained the flame of hope alive throughout the ordeal. As he went to his lodgings for the night, he was well aware that the most difficult portion was still ahead of him. The war was about to start, and he had the key to the future of his city and the lives of his people in his hands.

Palmer's day in Washington had been filled with a flurry of action on every front. She had poured a lot of time into evaluating the information, breaking down the enemy's plan, and speculating on what their next move might be. Her views had proven to be extremely helpful, helping to shape the United States' reaction to the crisis. She was about ready to call it a night, but she was well aware that the real fight had just begun. The chessboard had been prepared, all of the players were prepared, and it was almost time to begin the game.

The plans that Yurevich and his team had developed had been carried out without a hitch in Minsk. They had been successful in planting the seeds of revolt, and their deeds shone like a beacon of hope in the midst of the difficult times. Their efforts to secure their release had just picked up steam, but they were well aware that the most difficult test was still to come. The front lines of combat were established, and each participant was prepared to do their part in this momentous production.

The day served as a prologue to the looming war, providing a taste of the drama that was about to take place in the days ahead. The characters had been presented, their functions had been outlined, and the stage had been prepared. As everyone across the world held their breath, the stage was getting ready to be set for the next act of this international drama.

As the night progressed, it threw shadows across the countryside that were drawn out and menacing. It was a false sense of calm, an illusion that belied the anxiety that had become pervasive throughout the planet. The echoes of the day's events resonated through the hushed corridors of power, with each one serving as a jarring reminder of the thin line that separated peace from conflict.

The night sky served as a canvas against which Moscow's cityscape played out like a kaleidoscopic light show. Sokolov was examining the most recent information that had come in from the frontlines while he was stationed within the strategic command center. Each report was a piece of the puzzle, and every particular was essential to understanding the greater picture. His eyes darted quickly over the multitude of screens, taking in the information while his mind worked through various plans and counterstrategies. Regardless of the time of day, the thought of going to sleep was the farthest thing from his thoughts.

Petrovich was located in Kyiv, and he stood on the rooftop of the command center, with his attention fixated on the glow of the city in the distance. The wind carried with it the ethereal noises of the city, a hint that life was in danger. He was prepared for the struggle, the violence, and the loss that the morning would bring. He was also aware that they could not escape the struggle and that it was a battle they could not afford to lose. He turned, the contrast of his shadow against the metropolis serving as a visual representation of his unyielding resolve.

Palmer resumed her analysis of the streams of information that were coming into her office while she was stationed on the other side of the ocean at the core of the CIA headquarters. She was in a race against time, attempting to anticipate the next move the adversary would make, and trying to gain an advantage in the game with high stakes. She was both emboldened and horrified by the realization that the results of her investigation may potentially change the trajectory of the conflict.

Yurevich and his colleagues were keeping an eye on what was going on in the nation that was their neighbor while they were hiding beneath the busy streets of Minsk. Their hearts raced with the same feelings of both terror and hope. They had taken a chance and joined forces with the Ukrainians, despite the fact that they were well aware that this move may end in their deaths. However, they were also aware that it was a price they were ready to pay in order to gain their independence.

While the globe teetered on the verge of war, the individuals in our novel confronted the challenges they were presented with unwavering determination. They were all a crucial component of the growing story, and their parts were essential to the way things turned out. As the night wore on, so did the tension, a tangible expectation of the dawn that was to bring with it the promise of confrontation.

As the night progressed, so did the anticipation.

As the hours ticked away toward morning, people all across the world held their breath in anticipation. The tension-filled night appeared to reverberate with the collective beating of the hearts of millions of people. The specter of an imminent battle had spread over continents, spreading a pall that made the night seem even chillier, the quiet seem even louder, and the waiting feel intolerably long.

The command center that Sokolov had established in Moscow was a bustling hub of activity. Officers, military strategists, and technicians moved with an air of urgency, their features tense with concentration as they concentrated on their tasks. Sokolov was an immovable presence in the midst of total anarchy and stood at the center of everything that was going on. His eyes, which were keen and still, took in the commotion that was going on around him. His thoughts were like a maze, full of intricate plans and options for every possible outcome. The clock was ticking faster and faster. Soon, he would have to issue the order that would catalyze a fight that would involve the entire planet.

In Kyiv, the city itself served as a symbol of fortitude and will. Petrovich, unable to sleep and steadfast in his resolve, gathered his senior commanders together to formulate a defense strategy for the imminent assault. They laboriously studied the maps, discussed potential game plans, and made preparations for the worst. As Petrovich took one more glance over his city just before dawn, his eyes were steely as he surveyed the landscape. The responsibility of command resting heavily upon his shoulders, he braced his spirit for the ordeal that was about to come.

In the main building of the Central Intelligence Agency in Washington, Palmer's office was illuminated by the icy glow of many screens. She had been up all night putting together intelligence and attempting to forecast the next move that the adversary would make. She was aware that any fresh insight had the potential to change the outcome of the approaching fight, but time was of the essence. Her exhaustion clung to her like a second skin, but she shook it off, her determination being fueled by the seriousness of the situation.

Yurevich's rebels girded themselves for what was to come as they prepared themselves in a hidden network of tunnels located underneath Minsk. They had set the wheels of insurrection in motion, and there was no going back now that they had done so. They were aware that the dawn would bring fresh difficulties, maybe even a head-on clash. They did not waiver in their determination, and their spirit remained unshaken.

As everyone throughout the world waited, the seriousness of the looming battle pressed heavily on their hearts. The tension increased with each passing hour, building into a tangible current that glowed with eager expectancy. The scene was prepared, the performers were geared up, and the world was on the verge of witnessing the most crucial fight of the decade for the first time.

The first glimmer of light from dawn was barely audible on the horizon; it was a gentle glow that appeared inconsequential against the pitch-black background of the night. Nevertheless, it was the first moment of a day that would be unlike any other, a day that would be recorded in the annals of history.

At this point, the command center in Moscow was a complicated dance made up of very specific actions. Sokolov, who was in charge, had an air of unflappable composure. He issued the directives, and the room became quiet as his voice reverberated throughout it. The final seconds were being counted down. The Russian bear was poised to pounce, with its gaze fixed on the Ukrainian territory.

In Kyiv, Petrovich stood amid his men, all of whom had lines drawn across their cheeks to indicate their resolve. He took in each of their faces, feeling a mixture of pride and anxiety as his chest expanded in response. These were his soldiers, and they were prepared to give their lives in the service of their nation. Petrovich addressed his troops as the dawn broke, his words acting as a clarion cry that reverberated across the stillness of the early morning.

When Palmer eventually got up from her desk in Washington, she did so with eyes that were tired yet awake. She had exhausted all of her options, put together the shards of intelligence, and anticipated the actions that would be taken. She was aware that the day that lay ahead would push her abilities to the absolute limit as she made her way to the director's office.

Yurevich and his squad watched as light crept into their underground bunker in Minsk as it was being illuminated. The calm was an illusion, a cover-up for the fact that a storm was developing beneath the surface. They were aware that the next day had the potential to expose their covert operations. Despite this, they were prepared, and their determination was unwavering.

After what seemed like an eternity, morning eventually dawned, and as its light spread across the landscape, the world discovered that it was poised on the brink of a massive clash. Each participant in this international drama readied themselves for the impending storm, their hearts heavy with expectancy and their spirits bolstered by resolve. The time has finally arrived. The dramatic event was about to take place.

The sun began to rise, illuminating the earth in a ghostly white light as it did so. The stage was now exposed, showing that it was going to be used for a combat of enormous proportions. Every participant in this international game of chess, poised and ready for their move, stood on the edge of the cliff with their gaze fixed on the approaching storm.

Sokolov was in Moscow when the sun began to set, and he got to see the city as it became golden. His instructions had already been given, and his troops were already on the march. As he moved his eyes towards the enormous displays, the strategic charts were a testament to the approaching struggle, and his gaze sharpened as he did so. Sokolov was prepared to perform his role now that the game had officially begun.

Petrovich, unshakeable in his will and unafraid of danger, put on his combat gear in Kyiv. The city began to awaken as the light of morning brought with it the brutal truth of the impending conflict that was about to unfold. He watched as his warriors prepared, the expressions on their faces reflecting his own resolve. The time for discussion had run its course, and it was now time to take action.

When Palmer arrived in the director's office in Washington, she had a very serious expression on her face. She then handed over the intelligence report, which represented the culmination of her labors from the previous night. The Central Intelligence Agency (CIA) was on high alert and ready to guide the country through the chaos of the global crisis. At its core, the situation required Palmer to be willing to walk the tightrope.

Yurevich and his fellow rebels escaped from their safe shelter in the underground in Minsk. They dispersed themselves across the city, mingling in with the populace while concealing the insurrectionary fervor that burned inside their hearts behind masks. They were aware that their acts may spark a conflict on the front lines of their own country. However, they were prepared to make the sacrifices necessary to gain their freedom.

The anxiety was apparent as people all across the world came to terms with the new day's realities. It was a day filled with waiting and anticipation for the event. The scene had been prepared, and the action was about to begin. As the countdown began, the major participants, each of whom was situated in their respective corner, held their breath.

As the sun continued to rise higher in the sky, the anxiety that had been enveloping the entire planet began to be penetrated by the sun's penetrating beams. Its luminosity stood in sharp contrast to the rising shadows of the coming battle; it was a sign of the normalcy that was swiftly disappearing despite the best efforts of those involved.

Sokolov was like a modern-day warlord as he surveyed his control room in Moscow. He was poised on the brink of warfare. The displays in front of him displayed the movement of soldiers, the ready artillery, and the bristling power of the Russian military. The clock was ticking. As he braced himself for the impending collision, his heart was beating at a constant beat in his chest, and his stare was steely and immovable.

Petrovich rallied his men in Kyiv, his voice serving as a guiding light in the shadow of the approaching storm. His remarks reverberated off the still structures, serving as a demonstration of their steadfast character. His spirit was filled to the brim with both a strong sense of responsibility and pride. He had done all in his power to have his guys ready. It was time to confront the storm at this point.

Palmer presented the Director with her findings and briefed him in Washington. Her voice was even and unruffled as she laid out the many possibilities, the various outcomes, and the important turning points that may change the course of the battle. Her remarks reverberated throughout the empty office, each syllable serving as a jarring reminder of the enormous stakes with which they were contending.

In Minsk, Yurevich and his rebels invaded the city while hiding their identities behind masks and proceeding with an air of composed resolve. Their chests tightened with anticipation as each passing second brought them that much closer to achieving their objective. They had made their decision, and there was no going back now that they had taken that step.

The stress steadily increased as the hours passed by likes a ticking clock. Each minute seemed like a breath that was sucked out, and each second felt like a pulse that was missed. The globe was on the verge of a massive upheaval, a tectonic movement that had the potential to alter the topography of the whole planet for all time. As the participants in this complex game braced themselves, the scene was being prepared for the first scene of a drama that would send shockwaves through the annals of history.

As the day progressed, it appeared as though the entire globe was holding its breath. Every passing hour brought with it an additional layer of strain as well as an additional depth of uncertainty. The bright colors of ordinary life were giving way to the gloomy tones of an imminent war as quickly as the canvas of normalcy was being rapidly replaced by the sharp lines of battle.

The command center that Sokolov had established in Moscow was a hive of activity. The flurry of activity and the sense of urgency in the air were both pointing in the same direction, which was the unavoidable truth of the approaching clash. Sokolov was an unshakeable haven of composure standing in the midst of the mayhem. In his head, he was playing out several strategic scenarios, getting himself ready for any and all eventualities. The time was getting close. The ball was officially in play.

In preparation for the impending assault, Petrovich and his forces were making preparations in Kyiv. The atmosphere was dense with expectation, and the eyes of every soldier became steely with determination. The words said by Petrovich, which served as a rallying call for his men, were still ringing in their ears. They were prepared to confront the storm head-on as it was getting closer and closer.

A frenzy of activity within the CIA had been set off by Palmer's briefing, which took place in Washington. During this time, decisions were being taken, strategies were being developed, and assets were being shifted. They had been whipped into a frenzy of activity as a result of the impending confrontation. Palmer was standing smack dab in the middle of it all, the eye of the storm, her thoughts a swirling cauldron of knowledge and potential outcomes.

Yurevich and his fellow rebels had managed to successfully blend themselves into the rhythm of city life in Minsk. Their task had already begun, and the foundation for the uprising was being laid. Their determination was strengthened as the day went on, and their spirits were kept up by the hope that they would soon be free.

The anxiety was evident as the day transitioned into the evening dusk. The stage was set for a performance of a drama that would have a significant impact on the development of history. The players, all positioned in their respective corners, were prepared. The chessboard had been prepared, and the pieces were in position. At this point, there was nothing to do except wait, and the anticipation was building to the point where it may burst at any second.

As the dusk turned into a thick blanket of darkness, the participants in this complex game each found a time to themselves, a period in which they could be alone and think.

Sokolov stood in Moscow and glanced at the metropolis that was spread out in front of him. The cityscape was a silhouette of black shadows against the fading light. The load of the upcoming days, which he was prepared to bear, rested heavily on his shoulders as they approached. As he switched his attention back to the displays that were lighting up the room, he was aware of the fact that the next morning's sunrise would usher in the beginning of a brand-new age.

In Kyiv, Petrovich stood amid his sleeping men, the features of his soldiers bearing an expression of grim resolve even when they were at rest. His thoughts were filled with a secret prayer for their bravery and protection at that very moment. He took a moment to stare up at the clear night sky, and as he did so, his determination hardened. They were the barrier that separated their nation from the danger that was rising over it. And they did not waiver in their resolve.

While in Washington, Palmer laboriously went through her notes, all the while her mind was racing with potential plans and responses. Her office stood out as a bright spot in the otherwise dimly lighted building where it was located. She was aware that the path that lay in front of her was perilous, but she was prepared to traverse it and ready to play her role in this international game of chess.

Under the cover of darkness in Minsk, Yurevich convened a meeting with his fellow rebels, and the sound of their hushed preparations reverberated throughout the silent night. Their determination was unwavering, and they did not let anything dampen their spirits. Yurevich turned his attention to the pitch-dark sky as they gradually receded back into the darkness. The uprising was already under way, and they were beginning to weave the first threads of their independence in the shadows.

The sounds of the approaching storm continued to reverberate throughout the atmosphere as the day faded into the darkness of night. The stage was ready, the actors were prepared, and the plot was almost ready to be revealed. And as the night became even darker, the world readied itself for the impending battle, for the approaching dawn that would herald the start of a new era.

CHAPTER 3 "ECHOES OF WAR"

The dawn brought with it an ominous feeling; its golden tones tinged with the shadows of an imminent fight that was about to break out. It seemed as if there was a silent drumroll reverberating throughout the lonely expanses of Eastern Europe; the early air was vibrating with an expectant tension. The day had begun, and with it came the next act of the drama that was being played out on a worldwide scale.

The story had just recently come to light in Moscow. A "special military operation" in Ukraine was reportedly about to be launched, according to an announcement made by President Putin on a national broadcast. His words reverberated throughout the command center, where Sokolov stood with his eyes fixed on the enormous displays and his heart beating steadily against his ribs. The game had progressed to the following stage. The front lines of the conflict were established.

In Kyiv, the men working for Petrovich had hardly had time to comprehend the news when the first symptoms of an attack became apparent. The far-off roar of artillery fire and the anxious mutterings across the communications system both pointed to one harsh reality: the invasion had already begun. Petrovich roused his men while maintaining a stern expression on his face. They were in the center of the storm that had just arrived.

The news of Putin's declaration and the following invasion produced a seismic shift in the mood at the headquarters of the Central Intelligence Agency (CIA) in Washington. While he was standing in the director's office, Palmer could feel the pressure of the news beginning to sink in around them. The initial response from the international community was condemnation, followed by the imposition of sanctions on Russia and the testing and formation of alliances. It was as though the conflict was no longer confined to only Ukraine but had instead spilled out throughout the entire world.

The situation in Ukraine became increasingly critical as the hours passed. The Ukrainian military was putting up a vigorous battle against the Russian attack, which resulted in some cities being besieged. As a result of the Russian invasion, the Democratic People's Republic of Korea (DPRK) and the Democratic People's Republic of Korea (LPR) guerrillas were encouraged to make their movements, adding another layer of complication to the already chaotic battlefield. In the middle of everything, Petrovich and his troops fought bravely and held their position, shining as an example of heroism against the raging tempest of the fight.

Yurevich and his rebels were in Minsk when they received the news, and they listened to it in horrified silence. Their darkest fears were fulfilled as the world they knew was flipped on its head. But a rebellious spirit burned stronger and hotter within each of their hearts. The conflict was taking place not just in Ukraine but also extremely close to their borders. The fight for independence had morphed into a part of a wider struggle, with the stakes being far higher than they had ever been previously.

As the day progressed, the sounds of conflict continued to reverberate over the whole planet. As Ukraine prepared to defend itself against the Russian invasion, the rest of the world stood by in startled silence, watching as the sparks of revolt added gasoline to the blazing inferno. As night struck, the sounds of conflict echoed through the empty plains, creating a gloomy symphony that was reminiscent of a world on the verge of collapse.

As the war carried on, it appeared as though the entire globe stopped breathing. Every piece of news that came out, every report that came in from the front lines, added another layer of complexity to the rich tapestry that was the war. The entire world was a bubbling cauldron of anxiety, and the suspense was as thick as the smoke that billowed from the cities in Ukraine that were on fire.

From Moscow, Sokolov saw how the operations played out on the displays in front of him, which represented the chessboard-like layout of the battlefield. His armies were making progress, and the cities of Ukraine were gradually taking on the terrifying crimson color associated with conquering. However, he was not surprised by the ferocity of the opposition since he had anticipated it. As he watched the battle play out, his eyes never left the action, but his mind was racing with possible methods and plans.

The situation was really serious in Kyiv. The Russian onslaught was unrelenting, turning the sky above into a nightmarish cacophony of screaming jets and bursting shells. Petrovich and his troops were on the front lines of the battle; their faces were covered in perspiration and mud, but their spirits did not waver. Each explosion served as a timely reminder of the cause for which they were fighting: their country and their independence.

Palmer's time in Washington was filled with a never-ending whirlwind of activity. However, despite the fact that the sanctions were having an effect, the conflict was not yet ended. The world's superpowers were engaged in a game of tug of war, which caused the ties of alliances and diplomacy to become increasingly frayed. Palmer's thoughts were a tangled web of potential outcomes, but she kept her attention centered on the developing crisis in Ukraine.

Yurevich felt his heart pounding in his chest as he and his fellow insurgents watched the fighting from a distance in Minsk. Their goal had taken on a new sense of urgency, and the stakes were bigger than they could have ever envisioned at the outset. Their souls were ablaze with the fire of defiance, and the atmosphere around them pulsated with an intensified sense of determination.

The conflict continued unabated as day gave way to evening and darkness. The entire world was like a chessboard, with warring factions moving their pieces in a dance of death. The echoes of battle were so loud that they could not be ignored, and they served as a continual reminder of the storm that had come over the earth.

In the cover of night, the battlefield came to life in a horrifying display for the soldiers who were there. The horizon was bathed in an orange glow, and the fires of conflict threw strange shadows on the country that had been ravaged. The only sounds that could be heard were the roars of artillery, the crackle of gunfire, and the distant rumbling of tanks.

In Moscow, Sokolov's face was illuminated by the harsh glare of the displays, and the screens' increasing red lines indicated the progression of his forces' advance. Each successful operation brought them one step closer to their goal; but the opposition put up by the Ukrainians was proving to be more robust than they had anticipated. It was a war of attrition, and every hour that passed added a new facet to the struggle that was unfolding before everyone's eyes.

Petrovich found himself in the middle of the conflict when he arrived in Kyiv. The once-familiar metropolis had been reduced to a nightmarish maze of wreckage and destruction, and the continuous thunder of Russian artillery could be heard in the air. In the middle of the mayhem, his troops shone as an example of bravery despite the fact that their faces were caked with perspiration and dirt. Every encounter was a fight to the death, a struggle to defend their territory against the invading troops.

While in Washington, Palmer spent hours poring over the most recent reports, her eyes following the gruesome specifics of the fight. In response to the Russian onslaught, there was a surge of fury throughout the world that manifested as demonstrations and condemnations. However, looking at things from a more macro perspective, the sanctions turned out to be their most effective weapon. Her determination to comprehend the complex realm of geopolitics got greater as the night progressed farther into the night.

Yurevich was in Minsk when he felt the reverberations of the battle; the far-off echoes served as a jarring reminder of how important their duty was. The Belarusian capital was a place where anger was building to a boil, and a covert uprising was just waiting to be set off. They had a one-of-a-kind opportunity to strike, to undermine the Russian activities from within, while the attention of the world was focused on the situation in Ukraine.

The night was lit up with the atrocities of war, and the sounds of fighting could be heard reverberating through the empty spaces. But even in the middle of the mayhem and devastation, the human spirit showed through the brightest. The entire planet was on the verge of collapsing, perched precariously on the edge of a cliff. However, despite how rare hope was, it continued to serve as the light that guided them through the storm.

As daylight dawned, it was immediately obvious that the previous day's events had left their mark on the planet. The echoes of the conflict from the previous night lingered, serving as a terrible reminder of the cruelty that comes with war. The hazy horizon conveyed a terrible narrative of a place that was under siege and of people who were fighting against an invading enemy. It was a frightening sight, a representation of the unwavering will to fight back against oppression.

Sokolov was in Moscow, where he was studying the most recent information that had come in. They were taken aback by how effective the Ukrainian defense was, which was not what they had expected at all. Every insignificant defeat, every red dot on the map indicating a Ukrainian stronghold, was a pain in his side. His mind was constantly preparing, analyzing, and weighing each option with the accuracy of a seasoned professional tactician.

Even if it was only temporary, the morning provided Kyiv some much-needed relief. Petrovich was standing on top of a building that was only partially destroyed as the wounds of battle scarred the once-familiar skyline of his city. His soldiers, exhausted but unwavering in their will, got themselves ready for another day of fighting. Their appearances conveyed remarkable fortitude and an unyielding will to persevere in the face of hardship in both literal and figurative senses.

When Palmer arrived in Washington and went out into the dawn's early light, she couldn't help but feel as though the weight of the world was resting on her shoulders. The news coming out of Ukraine depicted a bleak picture. Sanctions were being enforced, but there were other factors besides economic pressure that would determine the result of this struggle. It was a conundrum of geopolitical maneuvering and strategic decision-making that had the potential to radically alter the established order of the globe.

At Minsk, Yurevich and his fellow rebels received a push in the right direction. The news coming out of Ukraine only served to reinforce their worst suspicions, and they were well aware that they needed to take immediate action. Their clandestine activities needed to destabilize the Russian military industrial complex and bring disorder to the established order. They were prepared to take a risk despite the enormous risks involved in the wager.

The daybreak was a sign of perseverance in the face of hardship; it shone like a lighthouse of hope in the middle of the storm. The echoes of conflict served as a sobering reminder of the price of freedom and the price of peace as the globe careened into an uncertain future. This was a crucial moment in history.

As the day progressed, the sounds of conflict could be heard reverberating over many continents. The tragedies of war had left their mark on the landscape of the Ukrainian battlefield, which was a macabre scene to see. In spite of the wreckage and desolation, the determination to fight on remained unwavering. The world's attention was firmly focused on the growing drama of daring and resistance, and the stakes had never been higher than they were at that moment.

From his office in Moscow, Sokolov continued to direct military operations as the battle progressed. The news that was slowly coming in were a mixed bag of victories and defeats. The opposition remained unyielding, and the stakes kept becoming higher. However, he needed to get to work. He was required to carry out the commands. There was still a long way to go in the game, and each piece on the chessboard had an important function to do.

Petrovich commanded his soldiers with an unrelenting tenacity right in the middle of the destruction that was Kyiv. The chances were stacked against them, and the danger was becoming closer by the second. Despite this, they did not budge from their position. Every skirmish they had with the adversary and every loss of life they sustained served as a harrowing reminder of the price they were ready to pay for their independence. Their bravery was their defense, and their spirit served as their stronghold.

Palmer was engaged in a struggle of her own there in Washington, and it was a strategic one. The conflict had sent ripples across world politics, and the shifting alliances and power relationships added complexity to a system that was already convoluted. Her part was more important than it had ever been, and the decisions she made had the ability to alter the whole direction of history.

Yurevich and his fellow rebels were the unsung heroes of this fight. They operated in the less-trafficked areas of Minsk. Their clandestine efforts constituted an essential gear in the machine, and their deeds were noteworthy in and of themselves. Their mission was loaded with peril, but they were aware that if they were successful, it was possible that their efforts may turn the course of the battle.

The sounds of conflict continued to vibrate throughout the day, which eventually turned into darkness. It was a stirring symphony, a demonstration of how the human spirit can persevere in the face of adversity. In the middle of the mayhem and obscurity, there was still a glimmer of hope that flickered like a single light in the vast expanse of night.

The arrival of nighttime brought with it a cloak of uncertainty as well as an eerie calm that belied the mayhem that had occurred throughout the day. The battleground, which was once ablaze with the ferocity of the struggle, now laid in an eerie stillness, with the smoke leftovers of the day's carnage remaining in the air.

Sokolov sat in Moscow and observed the night as the events of the previous day continued to swirl in his head. In spite of the defeats, he was well aware that the battle was not yet finished. His fingers moved slowly over the flashing screens as he planned the next move, like a chess grandmaster strategically repositioning his pieces across the board. Although the sound of gunshots was no longer audible, Sokolov continued to hear the music of battle in his imagination.

Petrovich and his guys were able to find some peace and quiet in the middle of Kyiv throughout the night. Their spirits were suffering from the burden of the struggle, and their hearts were sad from the losses that had occurred throughout the day. Each lost friend and each scar engraved onto the face of their city was a monument to their determination to fight back against the enemy. They were able to draw courage from the fact that they were together, which served as a ray of light amidst the darkness.

While in Washington, Palmer gained a greater understanding of the intricate realm of international politics. The international community's strong criticism of the Russian attack was an essential component, and the sanctions were starting to demonstrate their effectiveness. She was well-versed in the art of diplomacy and understood the significance of the complex web of alliances and agreements that molded the course of history.

In preparation for what was to come, Yurevich's rebels in Minsk took a number of precautions. Their covert actions, which took place in the background of the broader struggle, were a ray of light. The night provided them with a cover of secrecy, an opportunity to disrupt the Russian activities, and a window of time to provide the Ukrainians, who were under intense pressure, some breathing room.

The eerie peace of the night stood in sharp contrast to the bloodshed that had occurred during the day. The night was a quiet witness to the echoes of battle. It was just a little reprieve, but it was enough time to catch one's breath, grieve, and gather one's strength for the next conflicts. Amidst the gloom, the spirit of resistance blazed brighter than ever, and the hope for a better tomorrow flickered in the hearts of those who were caught in the raging maelstrom of the fight.

In sharp contrast to the frenetic activity that had been going on during the day, the nighttime hours brought a false sense of tranquility. Every nook and cranny of the battlefield, every face, and every murmured had stories of the conflict that reverberated across the land.

Sokolov was unable to find any peace or quiet in the Kremlin. His gaze traveled through the satellite photographs, reports, and latest developments. Every piece of information provided a clue or a suggestion that pointed him in the direction of the mystery he needed to unravel. His thoughts were constantly weaving different plans and scenarios, and he was always ready for any surprises that the conflict may throw his way. The reverberations of his clandestine conflict could be heard throughout the gloomy halls of the military command center.

Petrovich, who lived in the bowels of Kyiv, acted as a guard over his hometown. His guys were worn out but unwavering in their determination to put up a fight; their resolve had not been shaken. He was able to see it in their eyes, the fiery drive and the resolute determination they possessed. Their uncompromising determination was the spark that kept the darkness at away and kept it at bay it did.

Palmer was engaged in her very own conflict amidst the hustle and bustle of Washington. Her fingers deftly navigated the confidential documents, photos, and transcripts in front of her. She was negotiating the perilous terrain of global politics while threading a fine needle. Her actions were leaving ripples that would shape the result of this war. Her actions left ripples that would shape the outcome of this fight.

Yurevich and his fellow members of the rebel group were the unsung heroes who operated in the shadowy parts of Minsk. Their clandestine actions provided the besieged Ukrainians with a lifeline and a glimmer of hope during a time when both were in short supply. Every act of sabotage and every disruption was an essential step in the resistance movement's campaign against the invaders.

The darkness gave way to the first light of morning as the echoes of conflict served as a gloomy reminder of the harsh truth that they would soon be confronting. Despite the fact that there was a lot of uncertainty, dread, and sorrow, there was also a lot of optimism. The spirit of resistance, the resolve to battle on, was the symphony that resonated throughout the black night, and it served as a tribute to the unconquerable human spirit.

The eerie stillness of the night gave way to the gruesome reality of the day as soon as the sun came up. The sounds of battle resounded with a fresh ferocity, a spectral symphony that signaled the beginning of yet another day of fighting.

Sokolov readied himself for the events of the day in the heart of Moscow, which is considered to be the city's nerve center. He stood there as the city was illuminated by the first rays of morning, his chest aching from the strain of the conflict. He was aware that the cost would be significant, the price that they would pay for this struggle. However, he was a soldier, and his dedication to his mission was steadfast.

Petrovich gathered his troops together in the middle of Kyiv. The break of day brought with it a refreshed will to carry on with the battle, a renewed desire to do so. In spite of the overwhelming difficulties, they maintained their stoic composure and stood tall among the rubble. Every new day presented them with a fresh opportunity to fight, to resist, and to recapture their city.

Palmer was knee-deep in the muck and mire of international politics in the Washington, DC power corridors. She was acutely aware of the significance of each and every action and choice. Sanctions were a really useful tool, and one can already see the results of their application. Her concentration remained steadfast, and she did not waver in her determination. She was resolute in her desire to effect positive change.

Yurevich and his band of rebels awaited the morning eagerly as they lurked in the shadows of Minsk. They were the invisible fighters of this struggle, and the repercussions of their acts might be felt well beyond the local area in which they were located. Every clandestine operation and every act of resistance was an important step in the progression of their fight.

The daybreak served as a depressing reminder of the brutal truth, with the sounds of battle ringing throughout the countryside. Nevertheless, despite the hopelessness, the spirit of resistance continued on unabated. The drive to fight, to resist, was stronger than it had ever been, and its reverberations could be heard throughout the halls of authority as well as the streets littered with wreckage.

The light emerged above the horizon, which resulted in lengthy shadows being cast across the damaged terrain. The morning appeared to amplify the sounds of battle, which provided a gloomy soundtrack to a conflict that had affected countries all over the globe.

Sokolov remained in the Moscow citadel throughout the day to see its progression. He had controlled the actions of his soldiers with the dexterity of a trained puppeteer manipulating the strings, and he had precisely arranged the movements of his forces. The day would bring more conflicts and struggles, but he was ready for whatever came his way. He was the unseen architect of this conflict, and his hands were the ones who shaped its trajectory.

In the midst of the city that had been ravaged by fighting, Petrovich led his soldiers into another day of resistance. The battle had left the city with physical and emotional wounds, but its soul remained intact. He moved freely among his soldiers, his presence a palpable source of fortitude for the group. His determination became more resolute with each passing second as the screams of his hometown reverberated through his heart.

Palmer confronted the challenges of the day head-on in the political arena of Washington. She was the unsung heroine of this fight because the judgments she made molded the way the world community reacted to the crisis. She played a high-stakes game in which the repercussions were very real, juggling alliances, negotiating, and punishments all at the same time. She was the diplomat in the center of the storm, and the repercussions of her every action were felt all around the world.

Yurevich and his fellow rebels were the unseen guardians of the dawn in the murky land of Minsk. Their operations had gotten increasingly dangerous and risky as time went on. Each act of disobedience was a tremendous echo in the wider war, and the impact of their actions could be felt all over the battlefield.

The break of morning signaled the beginning of yet another day spent engulfed in conflict. The echoes of the fight could be heard for miles around, serving as a shiver-inducing reminder of the terrible truth. But in the middle of the din of battle, a symphony of resistance continued to play, and its rebellious notes reverberated throughout the ruined landscape, serving as a glimmer of hope in the midst of the mayhem.

While the echoes of conflict reverberated with a renewed vigor, the rising sun threw lengthy shadows across the battlegrounds that had been scarred. Scars and tales of the fight were painted on the terrain in every nook and cranny of the country, creating a gloomy scene that gave witness to the never-ending conflict.

Sokolov was located in the middle of Moscow, and he was grimly determined as he examined the morning's reports. His eyes traveled across the battlefield, following the movements of his soldiers while his thoughts raced forward to the conflicts that would unfold later that day. His command room was an impenetrable bastion of stillness, and every action he took was a well-considered part in this war dance. The implications of the decisions made during the day weighed heavily in the air, with each command having the potential to change the course of the fight.

In the middle of the destruction in Kyiv, Petrovich shone as a symbol of fortitude and determination. As the sun began to rise, his stubborn expression was a reflection of the unyielding spirit of his hometown. The sight of their leader being unshaken in the face of challenges bolstered the morale of the soldiers under his leadership, who gained strength from his unwavering determination. They were prepared for another day of fighting when morning broke, and the spirit of their readiness reverberated through the streets of the city that had been ravaged by the conflict.

In Washington, where Palmer was located, the day had already started for him in the still early hours of the morning. Her every choice reverberated in the international community's reaction to the crisis, and she had to weave a complicated web of talks, sanctions, and alliances. She was the hidden defender of world peace, and the measures she took shaped the path that this conflict took in ways that were not immediately apparent.

Yurevich and the other members of his rebel group were the unsung heroes of the morning in Minsk. Their stealthy and audacious acts caused a ripple effect that was felt well beyond their immediate neighborhood. Every act of resistance, every clandestine activity, was a blow dealt to the invaders and a step in the direction of their overarching objective.

The sounds of combat were increasingly audible as the morning progressed. Nevertheless, a symphony of resistance could be heard resonating across the region despite the chaos. In the middle of all the mayhem, it shone like a ray of light, testifying to the tenacity of the human spirit. The conflict was far from ended, but the echoes of resistance were distinct and determined; they were a potent symphony among the echoes of war.

As the morning continued, the echoes of battle, the unrelenting symphony of struggle, resonated throughout the terrain. The sun, which was ascending higher in the sky, put a harsh light over the battlegrounds, which brought the terrible reality of war into sharp contrast with its surroundings.

Sokolov, an experienced general, prepared himself for the impending assault within the citadel of Moscow. His intense gaze followed the progression of his troops over the interactive map that was sprawled out in front of him. Every choice he made and every command he gave influenced the direction the battle would go from that point on. His command area served as his stronghold and the strategic war room from which he supervised the progression of the conflict.

Petrovich gathered his troops in the ruined center of Kyiv, serving as a guiding light of unwavering determination among the upheaval. The sight of their commander being unshaken in the face of challenges inspired his followers to fight harder. His uncompromising energy reverberated throughout the city, reverberating along war-torn streets and into the hearts of the city's citizens who were already struggling. The resounding examples of his unflinching passion and unyielding drive infused the city with a fresh burst of energy.

Palmer maneuvered the pieces on her chessboard in the Washington, DC political arena with pinpoint accuracy and farsighted strategic acumen. Her day consisted entirely of non-stop meetings, negotiations, and conversations with other people. Each choice she made had far-reaching repercussions, having an effect not just on the conflict but also on the precarious equilibrium of political power on a worldwide scale. Her efforts reverberated across seas and continents, making her the unseen hand that guided the response of the world community to the crisis.

Yurevich and his gang of rebels worked covertly throughout Minsk, attacking when and where they were least likely to be discovered. Each clandestine operation that they were able to carry out was an audacious act of defiance that served as evidence of their resiliency. Their acts caused ripples that eventually became waves, which in turn impacted the broader dynamics of the battle. These ripples were heard far and wide.

The sounds of fighting were increasingly audible throughout the day as it progressed. The ominous beat that served as the soundtrack to the struggle permeated the atmosphere. Despite this, the symphony of resistance soared to a high and powerful pitch despite all the noise. It was a song of defiance that filled every heart and reverberated throughout every nook and cranny of the combat zone. It was a monument to the resiliency of the human race.

The echoes of battle became louder as the day carried on, and the symphony of warfare became more turbulent as the day progressed. The grim realities of war were brought into stark relief as the sun rose higher in the sky and sent its unyielding rays across the landscape.

Within the guarded walls of his command center in Moscow, General Sokolov maintained a stony face, and the eyes that betrayed nothing of the swirl of ideas within his mind were his trademark trait. He laboriously examined the troop movements and strategic locations depicted on the battle map, formulating and rewriting plans as the situation on the ground progressed. He sat bent over the map with his knees drawn up to his chest. His game of chess was a high-stakes affair in which people's lives were on the line, and the consequences of every move he made might be felt all across the battlefield.

Petrovich maintained a watchful stance among his fellow soldiers in the besieged city of Kyiv. The harshness of the reality of their predicament increased with the passage of each additional hour. However, it appeared that Petrovich's obstinate attitude was growing stronger. He rallied his men, instilling a spirit of resolve in them that rang through the heart of the city, and its vibration was felt in every area of the capital that was under siege.

Palmer was the hidden force behind the formulation of the worldwide reaction to the struggle that was taking place in Washington. She was waging a different type of battle from the sanctuaries of the State Department; one that was political in nature, plagued with the complexities of international diplomacy and the repercussions it had on the whole world. Her choices had repercussions on the global stage, where they affected both allies and opponents equally.

During this time, Yurevich and his band of insurgents continued to make progress with their uprising in the shadows of Minsk. Every single activity and every single act of disobedience made a significant contribution to the overarching conflict. Their deeds reverberated well beyond the bounds of the city, giving people who were engulfed in the conflict reason to have hope and inciting them to fight back against it.

The echoes of battle became louder and more intense as the afternoon shadows grew longer. The weight of the fight was palpable in the air as it grew heavier. The symphony of resistance, however, continued to play its defiant song in spite of the overwhelming cacophony. Its echoes were echoing louder than ever before, which is a monument to the unconquerable human spirit.

The sounds of battle were both more audible and more disturbing as the day progressed. The sun, which was now positioned quite low in the sky, threw a tone over the battlefield that resembled a sickening orange. Under this relentless light, the brutal facts of war were laid clear; the wounds of struggle were engraved deeply into the soil and into the people who lived there.

The command center run by General Sokolov in Moscow was buzzing with a tight and agitated atmosphere. There was a steady stream of dispatches coming in from the front lines, each one bearing the palpable weight of the fight with them. In spite of the raging storm, Sokolov kept his composure and focused his keen eyes on the intricate battle map that was sprawled out in front of him. Every choice he made had repercussions throughout the whole battlefield and had an effect on the lives of hundreds of soldiers who were under his command.

Petrovich gathered his forces in the middle of Kyiv, his determination unflinching the entire time. His presence was felt throughout the city, and it radiated an air of unyielding resolve that could be felt by all. Petrovich's determination appeared to only strengthen as the precariousness of the situation increased. His moral fortitude was like a resounding echo that resonated throughout the city, instilling bravery and resiliency in the hearts of his troops.

In the meantime, Palmer was able to successfully traverse the treacherous terrain of international politics from Washington. She led the international reaction to the war from her office, and the repercussions of her actions were felt all around the world. Each choice she took held weight and ramifications that extended well beyond the scope of the current crisis, and they would have an effect on the way politics would develop in the future on a global scale.

Yurevich and his band of rebels carried out their operations in Minsk from the cover of the night, and the effects of their acts were felt across the battle. Their defiance was an echo that spread well beyond the bounds of the city, which inspired hope and resistance among those who heard it. They persisted in their efforts despite the dangers, knowing that each act of defiance dealt a huge blow to the invaders.

It was getting darker, yet the sounds of battle continued to reverberate throughout the area, creating a tense and unsettling background score. Nevertheless, in the middle of this gloomy symphony, the tune of resistance continued to resound, reverberating through the hearts and minds of those who were caught up in the battle. It was a tremendous chant that held its own against the backdrop of conflict, which is a monument to the enduring resolve to fight for freedom and justice. The determination of the human spirit was a forceful refrain that held its own.

Long shadows were produced by the echoes of war, and they danced with the wavering light of the lowering sun as the dusk descended like a veil over the region that was in conflict. The battlefield was a tapestry of struggle and turmoil, the awful spectacle of war exposed bare beneath the growing darkness of the sky.

General Sokolov conducted his reconnaissance of the conflict zone while stationed in Moscow's fortified command center made of steel. His sharp eyes, honed by a seemingly endless string of battles, darted across the enormous war map that was set out in front of him. Every alteration in the movement of troops and every little variation in the power balance was reflected in the judgments he made regarding strategy. His directives resounded over the wide expanses, influencing the movement of the battle in a variety of significant ways.

Commander Petrovich continued to instill hope in his besieged soldiers as they were stationed in the damaged center of Kyiv. The unyielding nature of his soul reverberated through the streets of the city, making his presence feel like an anchor in the middle of the mayhem. His rallying screams went out in the nighttime air like a clarion cry to resistance, and the echoes stirred bravery in the hearts of his soldiers as well as the city's remaining citizens.

Palmer was deep in the maze-like realm of international diplomacy, which was located in Washington, which was located across the Atlantic. Her choices sent shockwaves throughout the world and had an effect on how other countries felt about the fight. This continued to happen with each passing hour. Her resoluteness, her commitment to negotiate the hazardous seas of politics, reverberated throughout the hallowed corridors of the State Department, motivating those who were in her immediate vicinity.

Yurevich and his band of rebels were undeterred by the growing darkness as they fought it off in the outskirts of Minsk. Their courageous acts of defiance rang through the streets of the city, causing disruptions to the activities of the adversary and boosting the morale of the Belarusian inhabitants who were under siege. Their bravery shone through in their deeds, which was a monument to their resiliency and offered a glimmer of hope despite the impending doom.

The echoes of violence grew into a deafening roar as night fell, providing a gloomy backdrop to the mounting horrors of the struggle. Nevertheless, the symphony of resistance carried on unabated despite the cacophony that was occurring. It was a rebellious tune that resonated profoundly in the face of enormous hardship; it was a monument to the tenacious human spirit.

The darkness of night brought with it an unsettling calm that was only broken by the sound of an occasional explosion in the distance, which served as a sharp reminder of the conflict that was still going on. The cities that were once busy now appeared to be ghostly copies of their former selves, haunted by the sounds of the combat that raged in the middle of them.

General Sokolov ruminated on the latest information that had been received from the frontlines as he sat within the guarded command headquarters in Moscow. Every choice he made was like throwing a stone into a pond full with conflict; it sent out ripples that had an effect on the lives of countless others. His directives, which were established in the sterile and impersonal setting of the command center, reverberated all over the battlefield and influenced the direction that the combat took.

In the meantime, in the center of Kyiv, Petrovich stood strong amidst the destruction, his spirit unbroken in spite of the challenges. His rallying screams, which were a beacon of hope and defiance, rang through the quiet of the city, and the reverberations strengthened the determination of his men as well as the remaining citizens. His soul was an echo of defiance in a city that refused to be shattered, that refused to fall silent. His spirit was an echo of defiance in a metropolis.

During his time in Washington, Palmer displayed a dogged resolve as he negotiated the perilous waters of foreign diplomacy. Her impact was felt all around the world, helping to mold the collective reaction to the conflict, and providing her contemporaries with inspiration. She never wavered in her pursuit of a solution that would bring back peace, in spite of the intricate geopolitical dynamics that were at play.

Yurevich and his band of rebels strolled eerily through the empty streets of Minsk at night, giving the impression that they were ghosts. Each mission that was accomplished without failure served as a glimmer of optimism and a sign of defiance that reverberated throughout the city and in the minds of those who were being persecuted. Their deeds were like quiet echoes in the night, providing as a constant reminder of their tenacity and resolve to put up a fight against their oppressors.

A single tune, which may be described as the music of resistance, remained consistent even as the echoes of the fighting from the previous day faded away, making way for the false stillness of the night. It reverberated through the stillness, serving as a powerful demonstration of the unconquerable spirit of the human race, which refused to be subdued and which also refused to be overcome.

In the depths of the night, the sounds of battle gradually dissipated, leaving behind a spooky silence. Under the icy, watchful eye of the moon, cities that once teemed with life now lay desolate and abandoned. However, behind this strange calm, the echoes of the fighting that had occurred earlier in the day continued to vibrate; it was a disturbing witness to the chaos that had swept across the region.

While stationed in Moscow, General Sokolov observed his commands being carried out on the battlefield in the form of troop movements. The strategic repercussions of his choices were felt throughout the war zone, and the results carried the weighty responsibility of lives lost and won. He peered out into the Moscow night as the last of his instructions for the day were being sent out, feeling the weight of the war in his heart.

Petrovich's voice was ultimately silenced in the damaged core of Kyiv, his rallying shouts being replaced by the far-off noises of the night. However, his presence continued to reverberate throughout the city, serving as a glimmer of optimism amid an otherwise desolate scene. He did ultimately give himself permission to take a short break, but the determination that was mirrored in his weary eyes reverberated into the stillness of the night.

As the events of the day's discussions came to a conclusion in Washington, Palmer discovered that she was embroiled in a complex web of diplomatic maneuverings. Her influence and drive reverberated throughout the halls of power, helping to mold the reaction of people all across the world to the battle. She was the only one in the office as the evening wore on, and the sound of her determination rang out in the shadows.

Yurevich and his fellow rebels vanished into the night in Minsk, and the aftermath of their acts could be heard echoing through the city's deserted streets. In spite of the stifling darkness, their echoes of resistance produced a symphony of optimism, which was a demonstration of their indomitable spirit. As they disappeared into the darkness, the echoes of their defiance rang out into the emptiness, serving as a pledge of their ongoing fight.

There was a deafening silence that hung heavily over the conflict-torn region as the night wore on and the sounds of combat gradually faded away, leaving behind just a hushed stillness. In spite of everything, there was a constant song that could be heard ringing out through the echoes of artillery fire and the yells of troops. everything tune was the symphony of resistance. It was a daring assertion of the human spirit that would continue to confront the dawn, and it reverberated strongly into the darkness, resonating into the heart of the struggle.

As a result, the sounds of battle eventually gave way to the stillness of night, providing a little reprieve from the unrelenting progression of the struggle. However, despite the fading of the echoes, the spirit of resistance continued to be strong. It continued to reverberate through the quiet as a continual reminder of the unwavering determination of those who were caught in the maelstrom of conflict.

CHAPTER 4 "SIEGE OF KYIV"

The unexpected onslaught of icy winds ripped through the city of Kyiv, screaming through its desolate streets and whirling around the shattered façade of buildings that were once bright. The city seemed to be holding its breath in nervous expectation of the impending storm that was about to rain upon it, and there was a pervasive sensation of foreboding expectancy that hung heavily over the metropolis.

Commander Petrovich was able to get a good look of his surroundings from the broken window of the temporary headquarters he was using in the middle of the city. His eyes were unyielding, and you could see the resolve written all over them. The city of Kyiv, which was also their city, was under attack. As the leader of the defenders, the weight of the blame for the city's eventual demise rested squarely on his shoulders. A mixture of fear, defiance, and determination could be seen on the features of the Ukrainian soldiers who surrounded him as they prepared for the impending assault. These men ranged in age from grizzled veterans to fresh-faced new recruits.

Erica Palmer was sitting at her desk in the CIA headquarters in the bustling center of Washington, D.C., with her eyes darting over several intelligence reports from a variety of sources. She was located on the other side of the Atlantic Ocean. Her head was swimming with ideas and hypotheses at the same time. The military strength of Russia was well-known, and their strategies were both successful and cruel. However, the fact that they were unable to achieve one of their primary goals, which was to take control of Kyiv, was inexplicable. Were there any other factors at play here? A more significant point that they were overlooking? She was tapping her fingers agitatedly on her desk, which was a quiet sign of the storm that was developing in her head.

The tranquility of the early morning hours in Kyiv was rudely disturbed as the thundering sound of artillery fire broke the silence. The city was pelted with bullets, which ricocheted off of the city's old cobblestone streets and sank their teeth into the decaying walls of the buildings. Petrovich showed no sign of fear when confronted with the relentless assault; rather, he did it out of a sense of empathy for the suffering of his city. The tremendous noise of combat was punctuated by the sound of his men's collective resistance as they returned fire from strategic locations dispersed around the city.

The ravages of war had left their mark on the formerly magnificent front of the cathedral that stood in the very center of the city. It functioned as a temporary hospital, and the reverberating corridors were filled with the groans of the injured and the hushed murmurs of the medical personnel who were working nonstop. In the midst of the commotion and mayhem, there was a young woman named Kateryna who worked very hard. Her youth was quickly being supplanted by the harsh realities of war, and she had gone from being a medical student to a combat medic. Despite this, she never lost her fighting spirit, and she never wavered in her determination; she was every bit a fighter as those who were fighting on the frontlines.

Palmer was lost in the complex web of intelligence reports and satellite photographs in Washington, which was located across the ocean. Her eyes were narrowed, and her fingers moved softly over the highlighted passages and jotted notes. Her stare was intense. The farther she dove into the reports, the more convinced she became of what she believed. In this equation, there was a factor that was hidden from view, like a specter lingering in the background. More than just a territorial takeover, the besieging of Kyiv served as a smokescreen and a curtain that hid the true aim of the conflict. But what exactly was Russia trying to accomplish?

A covert gathering was taking place in the venerable halls of the Kremlin in Moscow at the time. General Sokolov wore a look of grim resolve on his face as he paid close attention to what his commanders had to say. The besieging of Kyiv was just one small component of the overall plan. The hidden objective was moving forward in accordance with the blueprint. However, he couldn't help but feel a little uneasy in spite of how satisfied he was. His senses, which he had trained to perfection, informed him there were wheels inside wheels. Things were moving forward beyond their ability to control them.

Petrovich took leadership of his forces with a zeal that revitalized his soldiers right in the middle of Kyiv, beneath a sky that was becoming increasingly hazy in the morning. His voice, which could be heard crackling over the radios, served as a beacon of hope and resistance for his warriors, guiding them through the chaotic environment. An impromptu command center developed amidst the ruins and fires that were raging, and Petrovich was the one in charge of coordinating the resistance. Each order that Petrovich gave was a resolute refusal to give up their city.

Kateryna put forth an incredible amount of effort in the makeshift hospital, where her hands became smeared with the blood of her fellow compatriots. As she ministered to the injured, her emaciated face was highlighted by the light coming from the flickering candles and the dull electric bulbs. She was able to hear the deafening booms of artillery outside, but this just served to fortify her determination. Each life they were able to rescue was a demonstration of their resiliency and a blow to those who opposed them.

While doing so, Palmer sat in her office in Washington and combed over the lines of various reports and transcripts. There was a pattern that was developing, similar to how whispers in a storm may be felt despite their intangibility. Her sixth sense, which she had cultivated over the course of many years of research and observation, told her that she was onto something major. Her fingers were flying over the computer as she hurriedly drafted an emergency appeal to her supervisor for a more in-depth investigation into Russia's geopolitical goals beyond the invasion.

The encounter was on General Sokolov's mind as he reflected on it in the seclusion of his study. Something was in the air, and there was a feeling that there was a hidden motive. The bet was too risky, the move was too audacious, and the repercussions were too severe for there to be any doubt about what the real goal of this operation was. It was required of him as a soldier to follow instructions, but as a man who had spent his whole life serving his nation, he had to consider whether or not such commands were wise.

The music of conflict became increasingly harsh and forceful as it progressed. Petrovich, who was stationed in the command center, was the one in charge of organizing the resistance. As he did so, his eyes darted quickly over maps and charts, and his mind worked quickly to comprehend various ideas and tactics. A sneaky counterattack in this area, and a calculated withdrawal in that one. He was the conductor of the bold hymn of resistance, and he was the maestro. Nevertheless, whenever there was a period of relative calm, he'd find himself gazing out to the east. Towards the country of his birth. Towards the lines held by the enemy. What sort of activities were taking place on the opposite side?

at the midst of the mayhem that was going on at the improvised hospital, Kateryna performed surgery on a young soldier. The man's face showed signs of having just left childhood, and his body was peppered with shrapnel. Because of the critical nature of the situation, her hands worked with the dexterity of a skilled surgeon, and she was able to put aside her anxiety and forget about her lack of prior expertise. The only thing that mattered at this point was the life that was hanging perilously by a thread between her palms. Not only was she battling for his life, but she was also fighting against the cruel conflict that had taken him of his youth.

Palmer's plea had been granted on the opposite side of the Atlantic. The formation of a task force was now underway. The fact that her idea was treated with skepticism does not change the reality that the facts cannot be disputed. There was more going on with the invasion than first appeared to be the case. In addition to this, she was resolute in her pursuit of the facts. During the time that she was getting ready for the meeting with the task force, the unasked question kept running through her head. What were Russia's true motivations for taking such a belligerent stance?

The only sound that could be heard in General Sokolov's study was the gentle ticking of the old clock that was sitting on the general's desk. One idea took all of his attention. Was he only a pawn in a broader game? A piece on a chessboard in a game of power that extended beyond the boundaries of nations? In his capacity as a soldier, he was frequently had to accept his position as a pawn in the overall scheme of things. However, the repercussions of this operation were far too great, and the cost was far too expensive. Because of his undying devotion to his nation, he was obligated to cast doubt on the tactics, justifications, and toll that this conflict was taking.

The wind picked up, bearing with it the smell of charred wreckage all around the city. However, under Petrovich's leadership, Kyiv began to mount a counteroffensive. His familiarity with the structure of the city, with its confined streets and districts that resembled mazes, proved to be an invaluable resource, allowing him to use every twist and turn to his advantage. They did not retreat and put up a vigorous fight against those who had invaded their territory. Petrovich, on the other hand, was aware that the city could not hold out under an endless siege. He required more time, and the strategy that he had devised had to be successful.

In the meantime, Kateryna's hands started to cramp as a result of the ongoing procedures that were being performed in less-than-ideal settings, which were taking their toll on her. But she did not stop, and she was unable to stop. She did not have the luxury of doing so because of the constant flow of injured. Every scream of agony served as a jarring reminder of the catastrophic circumstances occurring beyond the makeshift hospital. She toiled relentlessly, and each successful surgery represented a modest win despite the overwhelming sense of hopelessness.

In Washington, Palmer's gaze wandered about the room, taking in the various emotions that the members of her task group were making. She was unmoved in the face of widespread skepticism and maintained her position. Her presentation of her data and her analysis were done in a methodical manner. She argued her case from each individual point. As she came to a conclusion, the conversation in the room came to a halt, and the weight of the repercussions of her statements hung heavy in the air. The conflict's stakes have just been raised, and the necessity of intervening has become more pressing.

When General Sokolov got back to Moscow, his level of irritation increased. When he attempted to challenge the strategies, he was faced with opposition, and at times downright hostility. He was the seasoned soldier, a guy who knew the price of battle and the carnage that it involved, and he was the one who led the charge. However, his worries were ignored, and his voice was lost in the din of competition for dominance. It appeared as though he was engaged in combat on two separate fronts at the same time. One against the government of Ukraine, and another against the leadership of his own country.

The days began to run together, which led to an increase in the amount of strain that Petrovich and his troops were under. The nonstop warfare was putting a strain on their resources and their ability to remain resilient. Despite this, the spirit of the Ukrainian people did not falter. They continued to battle because they believed in their cause and because they loved their country; this kept them hopeful. But Petrovich was aware that optimism alone was not sufficient; they need a breakthrough. And in order to do so, he had to put his money where his mouth was and devise a risky strategy that had the potential to either reverse the tide in their favor or seal their doom.

Kateryna had the impression that the number of people who were hurt was infinite. She couldn't allow herself to get overwhelmed by the gravity of the situation, and she couldn't allow herself to give in to the hopelessness that threatened to consume her. The young soldier who was currently under her care was struggling to breathe. Her hands moved with the efficiency that came from years of skill, while her mind pushed aside the tiredness to concentrate entirely on the activity at hand. Every beating of his heart was a pledge, and every gasp for air was a plea. A prayer not just for one's own survival but also for one's own tranquility.

Palmer was confronted with challenging issues, confusion, and doubt. However, she did not back down from her position and steadfastly defended it while fighting vehemently for her beliefs. She noticed that the uncertainty in their eyes was diminishing and being replaced with an increasing sense of comprehension with each new piece of information and argument that she presented. The understanding that Russia's invasion was not only an act of aggression but rather a meticulously planned strategy for something far more ominous than an act of violence alone.

Sokolov was thinking about picking up the bright red phone that was sitting on his desk and making the call that may potentially alter everything. It posed a threat to the established order, which was a danger. But he was willing to take the danger in order to protect the lives of his men and the future of his country. His palm was hovering over the phone as his mind raced through the various outcomes that may occur. At long last, after taking a few deep breaths, he went ahead and picked up the phone. He had made his decision.

The strategy that Petrovich came up with was extremely risky and bold at the same time. A covert operation with the goal of disrupting the supply routes used by the Russian military. His strategy took form more clearly with each passing hour. Each man was aware of the potential consequences, as well as the dangers involved. In spite of this, not a single guy flinched, and not a single voice trembled. Petrovich could not have been more pleased with the performance of his soldiers.

When a sharp yell from the front entry caught Kateryna's attention, she had just finished her procedure in the makeshift hospital where it was taking place. It was a young lad, no older than fifteen years old at the most. He pressed a rag-torn piece of fabric to his arm while blood oozed from the cracks in his fingers. His eyes had a haunting look to them, which served as a vivid reminder of the innocence that had been lost during the war. It broke Kateryna's heart to see him in such a state, and she hurried to be at his side.

When Palmer returned to the situation room in Washington, he saw that the atmosphere was changing. Skepticism was eventually replaced by reluctance and acceptance of the situation. As she came to the end of her presentation, she saw that the audience members' eyes had a hint of optimism. The hope that they could make a difference and stop something terrible from happening before it was too late.

The tension was palpable throughout Sokolov's talk with his unknown acquaintance. Sokolov was subjected to veiled threats as well as efforts at intimidation, but he remained unmoved. His determination was just as unshakeable as his faith in the responsibility he owed to his fellow soldiers and to his country. After hanging up, he immediately felt as though a weight had been lifted off his shoulders. Regardless of the result, he was confident that he had made the correct decision.

As darkness fell, Petrovich's troops began their covert operation by sneaking out of the compound. Even when the cold penetrated their garments, they did not budge from their stance. They navigated their way across the dangerous terrain using only the dim stars in the sky and their iron-clad determination as their sole guides. They were armed with information from their ground sources and their hearts were bursting with determination.

In Kyiv, Kateryna persevered with her labor, unflinching in both her hands and her soul. The young man, who had just turned 13, had reached a point of stability. However, there were others, a never-ending stream of bodies that were injured and beaten and need her assistance. As she walked from one patient to another, she was able to sense the pressure that came with her profession. She was not only a healer, but also a symbol of hope in the city that had been decimated by the war.

Within the intelligence community, a frenzy of activity was created as a direct result of Palmer's research. Every government agency, including the CIA, FBI, Pentagon, and White House, was on high alert. There were meetings, and strategies for potential outcomes were developed. The general opinion was that they couldn't afford to wait around and observe what happened. It was imperative that steps be taken at this very moment.

Sokolov, too, was geared up and ready for action within the spartan confines of his office. His words had set in motion a chain reaction that had started a chain of events that had the potential to change the way the war was going. He organized his forces and rallied them in preparation for what was to come. He could see the ferocity and resolve in their eyes as they fought for their homeland.

The clandestine operation had begun, and Petrovich's men were stealthily making their way across the snow-covered countryside. With each new step, they moved closer to their objective, which was a critical supply line that the Russians relied greatly on. If they were successful, they would be able to stymie the efforts of the adversary and afford their compatriots in Kyiv some much-needed extra time. Under the frigid gaze of the winter moon, the Ukrainians moved with pinpoint accuracy despite the fact that the mission was laden with danger. Their determination did not falter one bit.

In the meantime, Kateryna discovered that she was back in the improvised operating room where she had been before. The previous day's shelling had been intense, and they were getting dangerously low on supplies. The air was thick with the scent of antiseptic, which mingled with the metallic aftertaste of blood and the underlying undertones of both dread and resolve. Kateryna worked relentlessly despite the continual whirlwind of activity that was going on around her. Her nimble hands moved with a life-saving rhythm of their own.

Palmer's disclosures had sparked a frenzy of activity on the other side of the world, in the high-tech corridors of the Central Intelligence Agency (CIA). In light of the revelations that she had uncovered, every bit of information and every scrap of intelligence was being reevaluated. Her notion was gaining support, and the higher-ups were beginning to believe that they were dealing with something more nefarious than a straightforward territorial invasion at this point.

Petrovich's company made touch with the adversary when they were operating in the frigid wilderness. Unanticipated, but not quite unexpected, a Russian patrol was spotted. The combat was intense, lighting up the night with lights that blinded people and roars that could be heard for miles. The soldiers under Petrovich fought bravely and matched the Russians blow for blow throughout the battle. After the smoke had cleared, it was evident that they had prevailed in the combat, although it was still very early in the conflict.

The sounds of gunfire continued to ring in their ears as Petrovich's troops, concealed by the darkness of the winter night, advanced closer and closer to the target they had set for themselves. They had prevailed over the Russian patrol in the conflict, but they were still a long way from their ultimate objective. The pounding of their boots on the ice ground was perfectly synchronized with the beating of their hearts. In the stinging cold, their breath turned into frozen mist, and their features were set in a grim determination as their gaze concentrated on the work at hand. They went stealthily, unfazed by the previous conflict, their spirit burning brightly than it ever had before.

Back in Kyiv, Kateryna's shift had gone on for another day than it was supposed to. The formerly distinct boundary between day and night has become muddled as a result of an unrelenting cycle of activity. Every injured soldier who was brought in was a jarring reminder of how high the stakes were in this conflict. After she had completed suturing a wound, she glanced into the soldier's eyes and gave him a comforting smile as she ended the procedure. These kinds of inconspicuous acts were what kept people's spirits up in the besieged city's core during the siege.

When Palmer arrived in Washington, he found himself engulfed in a sea of maps, satellite photographs, and intelligence files. Her workstation was a jumbled mess of strewn papers and shards of knowledge that only she could put together. She had labored assiduously, each fresh piece of data lending credence to her idea. The atmosphere in the room radiated with an overwhelming feeling of time pressure. If she was right in her suspicions, then the situation was far more catastrophic than anybody could have anticipated.

During this time, Sokolov and the other members of his squad were currently plotting their next move in a safe area. His comments were delivered with a gloomy resolve, and he did not break eye contact as he spoke. The Russian onslaught had been terrible, but it had also stoked a fire among his people to fight back against the invaders. They were prepared for battle, and they intended to oppose the invader with everything they had until their very last breath.

The war's effects were being felt all around the world, with each individual occurrence acting as a pebble in a much greater body of water. As events progressed, it became clear that the Siege of Kyiv was more than just a fight; rather, it was developing into a challenge to the human will and the tenacity of the people involved.

Petrovich's crew moved closer during the cover of darkness toward their objective, which was a large supply store that was well guarded by Russian soldiers. Even at this late hour, the property bustled with activity, giving the impression of a massive monster. It was fortified, and there were troops patrolling the perimeter; this served as a jarring reminder of the tremendous undertaking that they had taken on. As Petrovich lay out the final particulars of their bold plan, the gang gathered around and held their breaths as if they were being kept captive by the freezing night.

Kateryna's hands were bleeding and her eyes were exhausted when she was in the middle of the city that was under assault, but she kept going because she had a great drive. The words of the city's mayor could be heard coming from a nearby little radio as it faintly buzzed. His words served as a beacon of hope and defiance against the approaching darkness. She could not allow herself to give in to hopelessness at this point. She preserved the spirit of Kyiv with each life that she rescued, which was a lot.

The bustle of activity had reached a fever pitch throughout the complex that served as the CIA's headquarters. The discovery that Palmer made had turned out to be an important part of the geopolitical picture that was emerging. It was no longer only about Russia and Ukraine; global forces were now entangled in a perilous game of chess, with Kyiv as the major battlefield. Kyiv was the key battlefield. Now that Palmer's superiors had heard her thoughts, they were giving them serious consideration and making plans to act on them.

Sokolov and his soldiers were preparing to mount a counterattack on the Russian forces while they were on the other side of the border. They had arrived at the decision to launch an assault on an enemy station that was essential to the Russian communications network via careful deliberation. The onslaught was sudden and unrelenting, which caused the Russian forces to be caught off guard.

The echoes of the ferocious battle tore through the calm night as the scent of gunpowder lingered thickly in the air.

The besieging of Kyiv was developing into a drawn-out battle, with the fate of the city hanging by a thread as the conflict played out on many fronts. It was a demonstration of the unyielding willpower of the human spirit, which refused to give up despite the impossibility of the situation.

While Petrovich's squad inconspicuously made its way towards the supply depot, the rest of the base continued to go about its business, completely unconscious to the impending threat. The troops were trading war stories, and their merriment could be heard wafting through the chilly night air. The depot was an enormous building that was stocked with guns, ammunition, and other supplies that were very necessary for the Russian soldiers that were stationed in Ukraine.

It started to snow very lightly, and the snowflakes were so little that they glistened in the erratic glare of the floodlights. The icy wind whipped across the desolate landscape, making the endeavor much more difficult than it already was. However, it did not seem to faze the team. Every action was meticulously calculated, from the first step to the last. The objective was to sneak inside the storage facility, ruin the supplies, and escape without being discovered. They faced a perilous mission, one that had the potential to change the course of the fight, and they needed to be successful.

Back in Kyiv, the improvised hospital was completely overwhelmed with injured citizens as well as military personnel. As Kateryna carried out yet another emergency treatment, her hands remained steady but her mind was a whirlwind of thoughts, feelings, and sheer resolve. The wailing of the sirens outside served as a brutal soundtrack to the wars that were being fought in silence behind the confines of the hospital. In spite of the difficult conditions, there was an obvious sense of solidarity and common purpose among those there. They were battling for more than just their own lives; they were fighting for their city and for their nation as well.

The office that Palmer had in Washington, District of Columbia, was stuffed to the brim with records, satellite photos, and maps. Her attention was riveted on the screen of her computer, which displayed a complex informational web that was, in its own way, a virtual battleground. The tension in the room could be felt by everyone there. Palmer was following a trail of digital breadcrumbs, which she suspected led to something of much more significance than the clandestine Russian actions she was investigating. Her intuition was usually spot on, and if she was correct this time, the globe was teetering on the edge of a disaster that reached well beyond what was happening in Ukraine.

Sokolov's Belarusian militia was wreaking havoc in the Russian communications outpost in the meantime. The unexpected assault was both violent and swift. Sokolov himself was in the vanguard of the conflict, acting as a tornado of rage and determination. His fighters, who were motivated by his leadership, followed suit, their insurrection serving as a ray of hope among the growing tension in the situation. Sokolov was aware that their minor act of resistance was just a pebble in the huge ocean of struggle, but he was also aware that even the smallest pebble might cause a tsunami if it was large enough. He was concerned about the potential consequences of their actions.

The Siege of Kyiv was taking place on a number of different fronts at the same time, creating an intricate tapestry of bravery, sorrow, and unwavering tenacity. As the city held its ground in the face of the unrelenting attack, people all around the world were watching and collectively holding their breath.

Petrovich and his men advanced through the darkening darkness until they reached the outskirts of the supply warehouse. The freezing air caused the guards' breath to foggy up as they patrolled the snowy surroundings while carrying heavy weapons. Petrovich peered through his binoculars at the security personnel while huddled in the underbrush. However, despite the fact that his heart was thumping like a drum in his chest, his countenance remained as icy and inscrutable as the snow that was under him.

He conveyed the strategy to his team through the use of various hand signals. They would separate into two groups: one would create a distraction on the south side of the depot in order to attract the guards away, while the other group would penetrate the depot from the north side. They were engaging in risky behavior by playing the game. With just one mistake, you risk being captured or much worse. On the other hand, the benefits of success were enormous. A much-needed breather for the Ukrainian forces would be provided by the depletion of Russian supplies, which would impede the progress of the Russian forces.

In spite of the screams of the injured and the near-constant sound of the sirens, Kateryna was able to maintain her focus in Kyiv. Her hands worked with dexterity as she stitched up wounds, set bones, and ultimately saved lives. Each person she helped was another soul that had been rescued from the clutches of war, and each patient she healed was another triumph over the invaders. It was her battleground, and she battled with every ounce of might and tenacity she could muster.

Palmer was working in the middle of Washington, District of Columbia, to piece together the various strands of her inquiry. She discovered an unusually high number of covert operations that could be linked back to Belarus, which indicated a considerably deeper engagement of Belarusian military than the Russians stated was the case. She had a sneaking suspicion that this was all part of a greater plan, that Russia was pulling the strings of this puppet play. She was unable to rid herself of the uncomfortable sensation that was nibbling at her stomach as she followed her digital footprints using her mouse.

Sokolov was in charge of the Belarusian militia, which engaged in a violent battle against the Russian army. Every shot they fired and every piece of equipment they destroyed was a declaration that they would not remain idly by while their homeland was used as a pawn in Russia's grandiose game. In the larger scope of things, the insurrection was rather little and nearly unimportant; nonetheless, it was expanding and gathering speed.

And so it came to pass that as the Siege of Kyiv escalated, so did the resistance - on the battlefields, in the hospitals, on the digital front, and most importantly, in the hearts of those who refused to be crushed.

The focus of the action shifted back to Petrovich and the other members of his squad. After receiving the signal and imitating a weak bird sound to perfection, the southern squad started their diversion. The monotony of the freezing night was broken when a grenade burst somewhere close to the south perimeter, first producing a low rumbling and then a high, piercing whistle. Guards rushed in the direction of the commotion as they heard alarms going off and saw red lights flashing in the darkness.

Petrovich directed his crew to take advantage of the distraction as the depot descended into anarchy. They were holding their breath and their hearts were racing as they scurried down the ice-covered ground. After a fast cut was made in the wire fence, they were able to go inside and move around undetected amid the shadows.

During this time, events in Palmer's inquiry in the United States took an unexpected turn. Surprise filled her eyes as she uncovered yet another secret operation. Her eyes widened. A well-known figure emerged, a high-ranking Belarusian military commander who she had previously investigated and found to be involved in questionable endeavors. Her gut told her that this couldn't possibly be a coincidence. As she dug deeper into the web of lies, the strands of her inquiry began to coalesce into a coherent whole that pulled her farther into the maze of lies.

When we checked up on Kateryna at the field hospital, she was knee-deep in a delicate operation. A soldier who had been severely injured by shrapnel was brought in, and his life was literally hanging by a thread. Despite the exhaustion that had worked its way into her bones, her hands were steady and her eyes were keen and focused. She reminded herself that the war had not been won just by their efforts on the battlefield as she made another precise incision.

The courageous Belarusian Sokolov was in the heart of a fight at the time, leading his troops in combat against a platoon of Russian forces. The ground trembled as a result of the weight of the war, and the night was filled with the sound of gunshots and explosions. His features were set, and a fire of resolve could be seen blazing in his eyes as he slaughtered opposing soldiers with a methodical rage.

The Siege of Kyiv was not just a competition of strength but also a demonstration of resiliency as time went on. In their individual capacities, each of these characters had a determination to keep going despite the challenges they faced. The beating heart of the resistance was stronger than it had ever been, regardless of whether it was in the freezing trenches of the battlefield, the demanding wards of a makeshift hospital, the digital warfront of clandestine operations, or the insurgent uprising in Belarus.

The Ukrainian detachment that was trying to infiltrate the Russian supply dump did so in a stealthy and quick manner while Petrovich directed their movements. His heart was beating as fast as a drum in his chest, but he kept his steely eyes fixed on the target. When viewed via night-vision goggles, the depot seemed to be a labyrinth of shadowy individuals running in the direction of the diversion that their team had made. They were successful in reaching their objective, which was a cache of ammo and gasoline. They immediately went to work with grim resolve in order to install the explosives after realizing that the high-value target was now within their grasp.

The metropolis of Washington, District of Columbia, was lighted by thousands of bright lights that stood out against the night sky. Palmer felt herself engulfed in the sterile blue glow of her laptop screen as her thoughts went into overdrive in the middle of this vast expanse of light and shadow. She was successful in establishing that the Belarusian commander in question was General Viktor Dukov. It was believed that Dukov, a previous ally of the United States, had remained impartial during this battle. The revelation of his involvement was a crucial turn of events, one that had repercussions that extended far into the future.

Back in Kyiv, the practiced movements of Kateryna's hands were carried out with intent and accuracy. This battle had an irreversible impact on the lives of innumerable people, and the young soldier who was in her care was only one of those countless lives. The cardiac monitor sent forth a faint but consistent beep, which served as a rhythmic reminder of the life that she was working so hard to rescue. Every stitch, every choice, was a confrontation with the menacing presence of death that loomed above her improvised operating theater.

Sokolov and his troops were involved in a heavy combat on the other side of the border, deep into the territory of Belarus. The sound of rapid firing and the whistling of bullets could be heard emanating from the densely forested region. He went through the forest as ghostly as possible, his face blackened with soot and covered in perspiration. Every time the trigger was pulled, it was a demonstration of defiance, a refusal to be dominated, and a rallying cry for freedom.

The stakes were extremely high, and there was very little room for making a mistake. The fate of the fight was decided in these decisive moments, and it was determined by the valiant deeds of common people who were pitted against exceptional conditions.

Petrovich and his staff worked with a ferocious level of concentration right in the middle of the storage facility. As Petrovich meticulously fitted each explosive device, he held wire cutters in his hand. It seemed as though they were an extension of his existence. There was no space for error, not here, not now; it was impossible. The sound of his watch ticking served as an ominous reminder of the time bomb that they were about to detonate.

Petrovich alerted his colleagues with a simple nod in the faint light, but it carried the weight of their mission since it indicated that the last of the explosives had been activated. They started to retreat, going back over their previous movements in an eerie stillness that belied the potential damage they had caused by leaving their path of devastation.

Palmer, who was located in Washington, D.C., pressed the send button with far greater force than was required. The information that was included in her email was intended to cause chaos in the highest levels of the American government. It was one thing to have a hunch about the participation of a former ally, but it was an entirely different thing to have the digital proof staring at her from the computer. She was going to agitate a hornet's nest, so she had a twinge of apprehension. However, this was a problem that had to be solved. No matter how uncomfortable the truth might be, it was her responsibility to find out what it was.

In Kyiv, the regular beep that came from the cardiac monitor had begun to pick up its pace. As she saw the young soldier's vitals soar, Kateryna wrinkled her brow in concentration. It wasn't long before his body started to rebel against the improvised procedure. She was aware that her window of opportunity was closing quickly. She took a deep breath before inserting the needle into his arm and administering the combination of medications in the hopes that it would stabilize him for long enough for her to do what she needed to do. Her hands, which were covered in blood and perspiration, did not shake at any point. She was not prepared to give up this existence in the face of the impending threat of death.

During the fierce battle that was taking place in Belarus, Sokolov's soldiers fought with a ferocity that was motivated both by their desperation and their desire for independence. The clearing in the woods had been converted into a battleground, and there, in defiance of the tyrannical rule of the invader, both men and women were willing to give their lives. But as the number of his colleagues continued to decrease, Sokolov realized that they required a lifeline as quickly as possible.

The cumulative effect of their separate deeds was having a resonant effect on a bigger scale, and it was irrevocably changing the course of the struggle that was playing out all around them. Everything was in its position, and the scene was ready for the dramatic conclusion to be played out.

Kyiv, the capital city of Ukraine, was bustling with activity. The population, while being worn down, was not able to be vanquished. Volunteers came from all walks of life and worked together to construct barriers, provide medical care for those who were injured, and disperse supplies. The scent of gunpowder saturated the air, and it was accompanied by a strong sense of both brotherhood and defiance.

The command center run by General Korolov was the nerve center of everything that was going on, and it was buzzing with incoming and outgoing messages, plans, and tactics. Real-time satellite photos, areas of heavy action, and military movements were displayed on the screens as they flashed. His eyes were fixed and unmoving, and they did not miss a thing.

While this was going on, Petrovich's hand was seen hovering over the remote detonator at the depot in Minsk. It wasn't dread that caused the sweat to run down his face; rather, it was anticipation. His colleagues were looking to him for leadership. He grimaced and nodded to his colleagues before pressing the button. Even from the safe distance that they were in, the explosion was quite loud. The darkness was engulfed in a raging orange fire that lit up the night sky like a blazing sign of their defiance.

In Washington, Palmer could sense the heat of the situation. Her email had been received, and her supervisors were requesting that she respond immediately. Conferences were swiftly organized, consultations with specialists were conducted, and emergency preparations were made. She was bearing the burden of duty, which was a significant burden. She was aware that the proof she had may swing the outcome of the war in either direction. She could only hold out the hope that things would turn out for the best.

Back in Kyiv, Kateryna was falling behind in her own personal fight. Her young patient, who was not that much older than her own kid, was quickly deteriorating. His breathing was weak, and his heartbeat was barely audible. Despite the fact that she could see the life leaving his eyes, she was determined to keep fighting. She took a long, deep breath, then mustered all of her power and labored assiduously to stave off the approaching shadow of death.

Sokolov discovered that he was at the eye of the storm despite the mayhem that was going on around him. There were signs that the Belarusian resistance was beginning to fail. Their ranks were being thinned down, and the odds were becoming increasingly against them. He was aware that they would not be able to maintain this pace for much longer. He did so with a sad heart and sent out a frantic request for further assistance. At this point, all they could do was wait and maintain their position in line.

The battle was being waged on various fronts, with heroes rising from unexpected places. These fronts ranged from the frontlines in Kyiv to the underground resistance in Belarus, and from operational theaters to the government offices in Washington. As the drama of the besieging of Kiev proceeded to play out, people all around the world watched with bated breath.

The rumbles of conflict continued to reverberate throughout the night, lighting up the acrid sky that hung over Kyiv. Every second seemed like an eternity, and every beat of my heart was a proclamation of my ability to persevere.

Petrovich and his men waited in the Minsk depot as their strategic objective was devoured by fire and saw it happen. A glimmer of light in the suffocating gloom was provided by their success, even though it was rather insignificant in comparison to the overall scale of the fight.

CIA analyst Palmer had just completed collating her results on the other side of the ocean. When she was about to send her results to the Director of the CIA, she was overcome with a foreboding fear. Now it was time for her to wait, with the outcome of her work's potential influence hanging in the balance.

In Kyiv, Kateryna arrived from her improvised operating room with the blood of numerous troops splattered all over her scrubs. Her attention was drawn to the young man she had labored so valiantly to save, whose chest was moving up and down with the natural rhythm of his breathing. Although the struggle had taken its toll on her, she was experiencing a wave of victory at this very moment.

Sokolov and his men were down to their last few reserves of

strength as they fought in the trenches. Their frantic plea for assistance had been broadcast, and its echoes were currently being reflected off of the desolate buildings and streets. They dug down, strengthened their walls, and prepared themselves for the onslaught that was almost certainly about to come their way.

General Korolov was conducting his reconnaissance of the city of Kyiv while stationed in the middle of the beleaguered city. His hometown. His followers. He allowed his sight to linger on the wounds of the wars that had been waged, fully aware that there were more to come. He was well aware that the night was not yet done and that the conflict was not yet won. But when he observed the city that he loved maintain its composure in the face of opposition, he realized that the people there would never give up.

They continued to fight despite being burdened by the war and living among the wreckage of what had been their life of tranquility in the past. Their unbroken spirits and unshakeable resolve are a tribute to the human capacity for resiliency, and each and every one of them is an example of that capacity. They stood firm in the face of the besiegement, ready to face whatever the coming morning could bring forth.

There was still a long way to go until the siege of Kyiv, which is the capital and the heart of Ukraine. The war cries of its defenders reverberated throughout the city, stirring the will of its inhabitants to fight another day and another battle. Each spirit, each heartbeat, was a demonstration of their resiliency and their unbreakable spirit in the face of adversity. They would continue to battle.

CHAPTER 5 "RETREAT AND REGROUP"

Kyiv was met by an unsettling calm as the harsh dawn broke, which was in sharp contrast to the clamor that had been there the previous night. Under the cover of the early morning mist, the Russian soldiers, which were once a terrifying flood threatening to swallow the city, had begun to withdraw from the area. It was a maneuver that no one anticipated, a planned withdrawal that left the Ukrainian defenses in a condition of apprehensive skepticism, and it left them in a state of disbelief.

General Korolov could barely believe the reports that were streaming into the command center where he was stationed. The Russian military is withdrawing their tanks, moving their men to the perimeter, and disengaging their advanced units. After being covered with red danger marks just a few hours earlier, the map was beginning to clear up like the sky in the morning after a storm.

Korolov issued the command, "I want all units on high alert," and his voice echoed across the room, which was otherwise silent. "This could turn out to be a trap."

Across the border in Belarus, the surprise Russian retreat had created a flurry of activity within the local resistance groups. This was due to the fact that the retreat was unexpected. Vadim, a freedom warrior from Belarus, found himself in the middle of all that was going on. He had insinuated himself into the 'Free Belarus' movement, which was a determined group of combatants willing to put everything on the line for the liberation of their own nation.

Although Vadim's first devotion was to his native nation, he saw the need of providing assistance to Ukraine. The Belarusian resistance is in a tough spot right now, but forming an alliance with the troops of Ukraine might provide it much-needed supplies as well as strategic advantages. After all, the adversary of his adversary was a friend of his own.

He was well aware that he was balancing on a knife edge. They would all be hunted down if the Belarusian authorities learned of their plans or if the Russian soldiers found where they were hiding out. However, he saw it as an opportunity and was prepared to accept the risk.

Using a secure channel, Vadim was able to communicate with members of the Ukrainian resistance and pass along vital intelligence on Russian army movements and their objectives. The intelligence was extremely helpful, as it allowed the Ukrainian military to accurately forecast the Russian plans and efficiently oppose them.

While all of this was going on, the CIA analyst Laura Palmer was drawing her own findings in the background. Something didn't make sense with Russia's abrupt exit from Kyiv, and we need answers. Palmer's intuition led her to believe that there was more going on here than met the eye, and she was eager to find out what it was.

After the smoke cleared in Kyiv and the withdrawal began to take shape, the field commander Sokolov and his crew needed some time to reorganize and recover from the trauma they had experienced. The fact that the devastated city continued to stand as a mute tribute to the resolve and fortitude of its people is remarkable.

Sokolov had the same rush of pride and relief as everyone else. They still owned the city, and it had not been destroyed. They had successfully resisted the onslaught of Russian troops. For the time being. Even though the conflict was far from done, they were victorious in an important battle today.

Kateryna's relief could be felt as she watched the retreating Russian soldiers from the vantage point of her improvised medical clinic, which was hidden from view. She had no idea how many lives she had saved or how many she had not been able to rescue. She was now able, thanks to the reprieve, to focus on caring to the injured, providing some relief to those who were experiencing the turmoil of battle.

A fresh wave of resolve surged over Ukraine as the soldiers withdrew from the city and the city itself began to reorganize. Every piece of information they exchanged, every wound they treated, and every life they preserved took them one step closer to achieving their ultimate objective, which was to protect their own property.

And in that common goal, they discovered the fortitude to continue the struggle another day. The day when Russia withdrew its forces from Kyiv would be seared into their memory, serving as a constant reminder of their determination, their bravery, and the indomitable spirit of a nation at war.

In the course of the day's progression in Kyiv, both the military and the civilian people of Ukraine started their difficult responsibilities. Soldiers worked tirelessly to fix their wrecked combat equipment, while medical staff, both professional and volunteer, tended to the injured. Damaged fortifications were rebuilt and replaced by the soldiers.

At the same time, military planners and analysts were poring through Vadim's information at a makeshift intelligence center that was hidden away in Kyiv's maze-like catacombs under the city. It was a shaky alliance that was forged amid the fires of battle, and it only lasted for a short time. It was more than they could have asked for in terms of the intelligence that the Belarusian freedom fighter supplied, since it detailed the troop movements, supply lines, and probable future objectives of the Russian forces.

The knowledge was quite valuable. It was planned out on large-scale printed maps and examined in great detail down to the minutest of nuances. Every officer and analyst who was present was aware of the significance of their mission; they knew that people's lives depended on the decisions they made.

When they returned to Belarus, Vadim found himself in a precarious situation. The clandestine get-togethers with other people involved in the resistance movement, the late-night radio communications, and the smuggling of supplies and weapons were now regular occurrences in his life. Every new day brought with it a sense of success, as well as a refreshed awareness of the enormous peril he was putting himself in by continuing to do what he was doing.

There was a frenzy of activity going on at the CIA headquarters in Washington. Every nook and cranny of the facility was overrun with documents, phone calls, and meetings that needed to be held immediately. Laura Palmer's face was lighted by the gentle glow of various computer displays as she combed through the information that was flowing in from a variety of different sources. Her gaze was glued to the screen the entire time, and her mind was racing to make the connections.

It became clear that there was a pattern developing, one that caused the hair on the back of her neck to stand on end. Throughout her career, Laura has participated in a sufficient number of clandestine missions to identify when anything was awry. The withdrawal of Russian soldiers from Kyiv was abrupt and perhaps even too abrupt. It seemed as though they had been dragged away for something else, perhaps something more important. However, what? Despite her hard efforts to solve the mystery, she couldn't shake the question, and it began to eat away at her mind.

A chill ran down Laura's spine as she sat in the stillness of her office, with the only sound being the buzz of her computer. It was as if she were standing on the precipice of a chasm, aware that the next move she made might either bring her to enlightenment or cause her to fall headfirst into the unknown.

General Ivankov's eyes, which were located in Russia, watched the newscasts in which it was reported that Russian soldiers had retreated from Kyiv. In the dimly lighted room, pictures flashed on the screen, but he maintained a look of stoicism, making his thoughts unintelligible. He was a veteran who had seen decades of combat, and the sudden withdrawal of support did not set well with him. He was a man of war. However, orders are orders, and he was a soldier to the core of his being. He obeyed the instructions given to him.

However, the truth was rather different. This was not a retreat; rather, it was a recalibration of our plans and a shift in our strategic approach. The Russian bear licked its wounds but was in no way ready to give up the fight. The weight of what was going to happen was something the general could feel in his bones.

Vadim, who lived on the other side of the border, was aware of the same fact. He had a close connection to the web of safe homes that served as the essential pillar of the Belarusian underground movement. As he went stealthily through the dark halls, he could sense that the opposition was getting more powerful with each passing day. Intelligence was coming in at a faster pace, supplies didn't change much, and most significantly, their spirit hadn't been dampened in the least.

Vadim had a meeting with the head of the community, an inconspicuous woman whose name was Katerina. Despite her little appearance, she possessed a strong energy. They were crammed into a small room, and the only source of light was a single light bulb. There were maps and radio equipment strewn about the room. Katerina's eyebrows furrowed as Vadim conveyed the information that he had gathered about the Russians getting back together. She was aware of what that signified, which was that they were preparing for another attack.

Laura's fears were validated while she was working at her office in Washington. Everything – the intelligence that was coming in from the field, the conversations that were being intercepted, the pictures from the satellites – went towards the same conclusion. The Russian soldiers were reorganizing themselves, most likely in preparation for a much more extensive onslaught. She was aware that she needed to communicate this knowledge to the highest levels of the United States government, so she dialed the secure line.

The statistics were being compiled into a report by Laura's deft fingers as they moved quickly across the keyboard. She felt a wave of fear sweep over her while she was sending it off to her bosses at the same time. The stakes were higher than they had ever been, with the specter of yet another Russian attack hanging over the situation and threatening to throw Ukraine and maybe the entire globe into even greater disarray. The echoes of battle were becoming increasingly audible, and the storm was not even close to being ended.

Colonel Andriy Rymarenko had asked for an urgent meeting to take place in the underground bunkers of Donetsk, which serves as a nerve center for the DPR. Unanticipatedly, they withdrew from Kyiv, and from that point on, every hour, minute, and second counted against their overall success. The lengthy, rectangular table was packed with the most senior military strategists, intelligence officers, and field commanders from Ukraine's armed forces.

He was a tall guy with grey flecks scattered throughout his normally dark hair, and he exuded an air of resolve that surrounded him. Rymarenko. It was clear by the look of his chiseled face and piercing stare that he had seen his fair share of bloodshed throughout the course of his life. He addressed the problem in a manner that was both calm and urgent, since he was aware of the significance of morale during times of conflict. "We've been granted a window, a reprieve. We have to look at this situation as an opportunity. "We need to get ready," he said.

His remarks carried a lot of weight in the stuffy room full of smoke. The outside of the city was completely destroyed, leaving just a skeleton of what it once was. However, the will of the people remained unbroken, and their resiliency shone brighter than any fire that Russia could light. They were the fundamental power of Ukraine, the driving force that kept them fighting despite all of the obstacles being stacked against them.

The Belarusian capital of Minsk, which is also the name of the city's largest district, was the location where the germs of insurrection were beginning to take root. Vitaly, our Belarusian freedom fighter, was stirring the pot of revolution, and his charm and daring were lighting a fire in the hearts of many people. In the face of insurmountable obstacles, the fact that the Russians had retreated served as a spark of inspiration and a glimmer of hope.

Always taking place in the dead of night, Vitaly's meetings with small groups took place in the bowels of dilapidated buildings, in the woods on the outskirts of the city, and other covert locations. Every time, he brought with him the quiet promise of a Belarus that was free; he conveyed the murmurs of resistance; he carried the whispers of transformation. Their numbers continued to increase at each subsequent gathering. Their determination became stronger with each secret vow that was spoken between them.

Back in Washington, the report that Laura submitted was raising a commotion. The news about Russia reorganizing itself was quite concerning. This wasn't a vacation spot; rather, it was the calm before the impending storm. She was ushered into a meeting with the Director of the Central Intelligence Agency, a stern and experienced veteran by the name of Director Harlan. The setting was severe, and the tension in the air was palpable. As soon as Laura walked in, the Director's penetrating stare landed on her, and his words carried with it the weight of the entire world. He added to her, "We're on borrowed time, Laura," which was a comment that echoed her own feelings exactly. "Time is running out," they said. "The clock is ticking."

In the days that followed, Donetsk bustled with a newfound vitality and activity. While military personnel worked diligently on their training, citizens helped in their own unique ways, such as by sewing uniforms, packing medical kits, and even preparing meals for military personnel. The initial shock caused by the withdrawal was transformed into a rallying cry for readiness and resiliency thanks to Andriy's remarks, which lit a flame that now coursed through the veins of the city.

The city was like a beehive, buzzing with activity and a common goal. In one area, a group of young people who volunteered their time quickly stacked sandbags to create temporary fortifications in preparation for the next onslaught. In another, medical personnel with tired eyes worked nonstop to treat those who had been hurt and to get ready for others who would sustain injuries in the future.

While Andriy was working to strengthen the fortifications, Vitaly was in Minsk stoking the flames of insurrection. As he conveyed the facts of Ukraine's resistance and Russia's short setback, the anticipation in his chest caused his heart to pound rapidly. The undercurrents of revolt were becoming a storm surge that threatened to topple the authoritarian authority that had captivated Belarus. This tide was shifting and it threatened to overturn the authoritarian rule that had gripped Belarus.

Vitaly was able to provide important intelligence to Ukraine by utilizing a dependable network of supporters. The routes that Russian convoys were travelling, the number of troops that were amassing near the border, and even detailed data about their supply network are all pieces of knowledge that may provide the Ukrainians with an advantage in the approaching fight.

In the meantime, hundreds of miles away in the heavily guarded hallways of the CIA, Laura was masterminding a geopolitical chess game with huge stakes. Together with Director Harlan, she combed through satellite pictures, ciphered correspondence, and testimonies provided by defectors in an effort to decipher Putin's next move.

Her deft hands sketched the shapes of Russian regiments on the digital maps, while her perceptive mind connected the dots and unraveled the web of information. It was up to her to foresee what would happen, to see into the void of the unknown and identify patterns, dangers, and possible courses of action. She was moving about in a sea of obscurity, and each step she took had the potential to alter the way things turned out in the long run.

The ringing of her phone startled her out of her musings at that moment. A secret transmission received from a covert asset located in Belarus. As she cracked the message's encryption, she felt a tremor of excitement go through her body. The data provided by Vitaly was an unexpected piece of the jigsaw for her; it was a wild card that had the potential to give them the upper hand.

While this was going on, the rest of the world stood by in startled stillness, holding its breath as they waited for the storm that was about to be let loose. At the same time that governments were jockeying for position on the world stage, the everyday people who were caught in the middle of the fight were preparing themselves for what was to come. The action was about to begin, all of the participants were prepared, and the sounds of battle were growing increasingly audible with each passing second.

As Laura's voice reverberated over the conference phone, a colossal screen in the war room of the Pentagon highlighted the faces of serious military people. Her tone was unruffled and unwavering as she related the information that had been gathered from the source in Belarus. They had the opportunity to swing the balance in Ukraine's favor and give the country a fighting chance, and the significance of this was quite evident.

Leaning forward, a general in the Army could be seen to have lines of strategic battle planning engraved into his face. His remarks pierced the air of tense anticipation that pervaded the room as he asserted, "We need to expedite our supply routes to Ukraine."

Back in Kyiv, in a secluded area of his office, Andriy was observed slouched over a desk, intently examining the information that Laura had forwarded on. His fingers traced the routes of probable Russian advancements and the areas that were open to being exploited. He was looking for the Russians. Even while the danger was still very present, they suddenly had an advantage, a narrow window of time to reverse the flow of the battle.

Makeshift drills were operating at full capacity on the outskirts of the city. Soldiers, their brows furrowed and eyes fixed, rehearsed shooting rounds, perfected their tactical moves, and surveyed the landscape as they prepared for battle. One could feel the underlying feeling of determination and resolution in the air. This was their home, and they were prepared to do whatever it took to protect it.

Vitaly, on the other hand, who was deep within Minsk, was experiencing the excitement of expectancy. The subterranean resistance organization was energized after hearing the news that the Russians had retreated from Kyiv. Secret cells all around the city communicated with one another using coded signals as they planned, strategized, and waited for the right moment to launch their attack. Their cause was given fresh life by the news of Ukraine's resilience, which caused their optimism to shine brilliantly in spite of the tyranny that they were facing.

Despite this, the whole globe remained in a state of anticipation. Everyone was focused on the East, where they were eagerly expecting the next move. Protesters flooded the streets of major cities in the West, their unified cries of defiance creating a cacophony in the public squares. As a result of the tightening of sanctions on Russia, economic conditions got more difficult, partnerships were put to the test, and diplomacy became like a game of high-stakes poker.

The pieces were in motion, and their subsequent movements were both unforeseeable and related. It was all part of a delicate dance, an interplay of decisions and reactions that would define the fate of countries; the next move that Russia would make, the answer that Ukraine would give, and the reaction of the rest of the world. And in this big scheme, people such as Andriy, Laura, and Vitaly, and even General Kuznetsov, played their part, with their actions causing ripples that would ultimately influence the path of history.

As the sun went down, spreading deep shadows over the territories that were besieged, a collective determination began to take shape. The echoes of retreat evolved into the drumming of defiance, a song of resilience that range from the war-torn streets of Kyiv to the resistance-filled cellars of Minsk, the headquarters of the CIA, and beyond afield. The conditions were perfect for a clash, a battle that would not just be about gaining control of territory but also over the fundamental meaning of freedom and sovereignty.

During the course of that evening, Laura went for a walk around her apartment when it was in the throes of nightfall. She was always on high alert, ready to spring into action at the sound of her private phone, which was kept in a safe location. In spite of the late hour, she was fully awake, her mind preoccupied with the complex web of facts, hypotheses, and potential outcomes.

She saw the map of Eastern Europe in her mind, with the pinpricks of battle, diplomatic maneuvers, and the invisible movements in power all lighted on it. She was aware that her assessments and suggestions, which would be sent via the CIA's organizational structure and presented to the highest levels of government, had the potential to change the dynamics of the battle.

Her shoulders felt like they were being crushed by the weight of that obligation.

As the night progressed, Laura noticed that there was a structure, an elaborate sequence that was buried within the mayhem. She was sure it was important despite the fact that it was little more than a thread. She began to weave her idea like a professional cryptographer, her thoughts racing as the parts began to fall into place.

Andriy, who was stationed on the other side of the ocean in Kyiv, was the one who was informed by his superiors that life-saving assistance had arrived from the West. When he understood the possible impact that this support may have, his heart began to pound with eagerness. It has the potential to change the course of the conflict and offer them a chance to fight back. In the midst of the harsh realities of war, it was a glimpse of optimism.

At the same moment, General Kuznetsov was standing on a hill that overlooked the nighttime outskirts of Kyiv. He could see the city in the distance. He felt a peculiar combination of admiration and exasperation in response to the city's steadfastness despite the fact that it was relatively peaceful. His instructions were crystal clear, but carrying them out was proving to be a difficult task. It had come as a surprise to him how strong the Ukrainian opposition would be, and as a result, he was being compelled to rethink his approach.

During this time, Vitaly was in Minsk meeting with the top commanders of the resistance. He then informed her of the information that he had obtained from Laura, and the three of them then crouched down together and conspired. The atmosphere in the room was charged with anxiety and the strain of having a common goal. They were well aware that they were playing with fire and that they were putting their lives in danger with each step they took, but the desire for independence and the opportunity to influence the destiny of their nation inspired them to keep going.

A weird and perhaps lethal ballet was taking shape despite the presence of the cloak of night and the strain of the battle. Each participant acted according to their own rhythm, and the acts they took determined how the impending confrontation would play out. They were all aware that the following few days would be extremely important as the sun began to peek over the horizon in the morning. Each choice and action would have repercussions that would be felt not only locally but also throughout the area and the rest of the world. The scene was ready, and all of the participants were geared up. Now was the moment to take action.

As daylight approached, there was a discernible shift in the dynamic of the combat. Over in Washington, Laura was nearly able to picture the complex web of power relationships, shifting alliances, and hidden secrets. She had a peek at the data that had been encrypted and sent by Vitaly. These documents detailed the formation of a resistance organization in Belarus, as well as provided information on military movements and vulnerabilities in Russia's strategic planning. Even though she did not yet have all of the pieces of the jigsaw, she was starting to get a better understanding of the wider image. For the time being, she communicated the deciphered information to her superiors while frantically typing with her fingers flying over the keyboard and her heart hammering in her chest.

Vitaly, on the other hand, who was now more involved than he had ever been in the Belarusian resistance movement, was caught up in a tornado of secret meetings and encrypted correspondence. The leaders of the resistance in Minsk, viewing him as a vital asset, met with him in the basement of an ordinary suburban house in Minsk to plot their next course of action. The room had an emotion that was a mix of nervousness, resolve, and terror, and it was palpable to everyone there. Everyone present was aware of the significance of what they were doing and the potential consequences of their actions.

Back in Ukraine, Andriy and his forces did not back down from their position. The Russian withdrawal provided a much-needed breather, and the defenders quickly took advantage of the lull in the action to strengthen their positions. As barricades were set up, trenches were excavated, and anti-aircraft missiles were positioned, the streets of Kyiv were bustling with activity and the air was thick with the aroma of raw dirt and cold metal. The city had been converted into a fortress, and its inhabitants had shown no sign of being shaken by the impending danger. Andriy's eyes traveled across the city that he had taken an oath to defend as a look of resolve carved itself into his features.

From his command position, General Kuznetsov observed the Ukrainian defenses with an expression that was difficult to interpret. He had not prepared himself for such a robust opposition. It was a struggle for him to balance his responsibility to carry out the orders given to him with the increasing admiration he had for the adversary. The resiliency shown by the Ukrainians was not only a challenge but also a demonstration of the power of the human spirit. However, instructions were orders, and he had a responsibility to serve his nation in any way he could. After stealing his will, he began the process of rethinking his plan.

As a sobering reminder of how high the stakes were, the reverberation from the earlier invasion could still be heard in the air. Every participant in this multinational drama was strategizing their next move and making their actions, well aware that any one action may tilt the scales in their favor or against another participant. They were fully aware that they were on the precipice of a moment that had the potential to transform the world as they maneuvered through the intricate maze of geopolitical plans, alliances, and betrayals that they were entangled in.

As Laura passed on the information, she experienced an uncomfortable sensation, similar to that of walking on a wire that was hanging above a vast chasm. However, despite the fact that she required approval from her superiors before moving forward, she continued to formulate her theories. The pieces were placed on the chessboard. Russia, Ukraine, and Belarus occupied their respective positions as the kings, queens, knights, and pawns on the chess board. Each nation made strategic moves in an effort to gain an advantage over the other. She was well aware that the slightest mistake may result in the utter destruction of Ukraine, the destabilization of Europe, and the strengthening of Russia.

Vitaly gathered with the other leaders of the resistance in the dimly lighted basement of the building in Minsk. On the scratched and worn wooden table, which was surrounded by mugs of iced coffee, there were several maps and rudimentary schematics of important places scattered about. They were deep in conversation, refining their strategies for an unprecedented onslaught against the dictatorship of Lukashenko, which was supported by the Kremlin. Their comments echoed off the old brick walls, filling the space with a cacophony of mutterings and hushed conversations that served as the background score for the uprising.

Because he had withstood the ravages of so many conflicts, Andriy towered above the other troops under his command. His enthusiasm was contagious, his determination was unshakeable, and his commitment was motivating. He did not address them in an authoritative capacity but rather as a fellow soldier, rousing his weary but undaunted troops with fervent speeches and words of support. An additional attack was expected, which caused unease, but the Ukrainian soldiers were able to form an impregnable barrier because to their sense of solidarity and their desire to defend their motherland. The air was thick with the scent of gunpowder, perspiration, and dogged resolve all mingling together.

At the Russian command post, Kuznetsov discovered that he was caught up in the maelstrom of war, which was not only the fight that was taking place on the battlefield but also the conflict that was taking place within himself. His instructions were very clear, but the situation on the ground was growing increasingly unclear. It was a hazardous attitude for a military man to have, as his admiration for the bravery of the adversary grew. The steady ticking of his fingers on the table's metal surface reflected the anxiety that he felt on the inside.

In the hurriedly constructed barricades in Kyiv, in the resistance cell operating out of a cellar in Minsk, in the labyrinthine halls of the CIA in Washington, and in the unwavering glare of a Russian general, the invisible shadows of the war were everywhere. As the invisible forces continued to alter the fates of nations and individuals alike, the next episode of this geopolitical play continued to develop, and it was getting dangerously close to the brink of a new global order.

Within the walls of the Central Intelligence Agency Headquarters in the heart of Washington, Laura's office was a beehive of activity. Analysts were rushing about the room, bringing in new reports and data as they went. Satellite photos, intercepted messages, and patterns all provided hints towards a more in-depth story, a story that Laura was gradually putting together piece by piece. the eyes hurt from the brightness of the white background on the computer screen, which was displaying secret documents and lines of code being processed by intelligence software. The only sound that broke the uncomfortable stillness in the room was the delicate clicking and clacking of her keyboard.

Back in the bunker where the resistance was hiding, Vitaly was hard at work putting together his message for the Ukrainian headquarters. They had been successful in penetrating one of Lukashenko's installations and had obtained information about a big armaments shipment that was headed towards the Russian soldiers that were stationed at the border of Ukraine. Every stroke he made on the keyboard had the potential to radically change how the fight would unfold. He was well aware of the seriousness of the information that he was going to transmit, and he carried the burden of the obligation on his shoulders with great heaviness.

Andriy was positioned such that he was looking down at a comprehensive map of Ukraine that was spread out before him on a makeshift battle table. It was everything there, down to the itty-bitty numbers that represented army movements, enemy locations, and supply lines. The information that had come in from Belarus had given his soldiers fresh life, and their spirits had been buoyed by the possibility of a change in the status quo. As he mentally prepared himself for the fight that was yet to come, his rough, battle-hardened fingers drew over the paths that his troops would travel.

Back in Russia, General Kuznetsov was struggling to keep his head above water due to his mounting concerns. The arrival of winter had a demoralizing effect on his troops, and his adversary continued to hold their ground. As he continued to review the most recent reports, the lively conversation coming from his command center became a monotonous background noise. The mortality rates, ammo counts, and resource use gave him a sick feeling in the pit of his stomach. Every single number, every single statistic, and every single graphic bears the gloomy imprint of war's harsh reality.

The influence of the geopolitical game rippled over a wide variety of nations and levels. The next move was being planned, alliances were being forged, plans were being created, strategies were being evaluated, and preparations were well under way. Unseen shadows continued to cast a vast shadow among the tension and upheaval, determining the fate of nations in a world that was teetering on the edge of total anarchy.

As the night progressed, it appeared as though the entire planet stopped breathing for a moment. Andriy, who was in Ukraine at the time, was standing on the edges of his camp and looking into the darkness that extended beyond it. The icy winds of winter nipped at his skin, and he could see his breath condensing into icy clouds around him. He could make out the silhouettes of his soldiers as they crowded together around the flames, the wavering light illuminating their features. They had been granted a little reprieve from the atrocities of war in the form of a fragile serenity. Andriy was aware that this calm would not last, that it was only a stolen moment that was destined to be shattered as soon as the sun rose.

Vitaly was sitting in the middle of a desolate woodland in Belarus, illuminated only by the glow of his laptop screen. As evidence of how frantically they were working, the room was in a state of disorder, with wires winding about and half-eaten lunches laying around abandoned. While he was deciphering the vital message, the flickering flame of a single candle created a series of shifting shadows on his face. Every press on the keyboard was like a hushed confession that was being transmitted to Ukraine, and his pulse beat in time with the rapid keystrokes.

When we last left Laura, she was lost in the complex maze of codes and patterns that occupied the CIA headquarters. Her attention was drawn to a dialogue that was encrypted. A high-ranking official in the Russian government discussing a strategy that did not correspond with their existing approach. The possibility of a more sinister drive or covert objective once more reared its head. An oddity that stuck in her head like a thorn, a piece of the puzzle that did not belong. An oddity that has the potential to shed light on Russia's genuine motivations for its actions.

While everything was going on, General Kuznetsov was engaged in a personal struggle within the Russian command center. The room was alive with murmured conversations, rushed commands, and the intermittent ringing of a red phone. Even though he was a veteran of many years of combat and had become jaded as a result, the tragic loss of life nevertheless affected him deeply. It was his commands, his plans, and his actions that were causing people to lose their lives. It was a price that he did not like to pay, but it was one that he could not avoid paying because he had no control over it. He couldn't shake the images of the dead, the gloomy look in their eyes serving as a constant reminder of the toll that war takes.

They were the pieces moving across a chessboard, and the world was the board. Every action they did and every choice they made would send reverberations across the fabric of reality, so determining the path that the battle would take. As they maneuvered across this hazardous terrain, their deeds, their victories, and their defeats would become the echoes of a conflict that had not yet revealed its full fury.

The city of Kyiv finally started to let out the breath it had been holding for such a long time as the Russian army began to retreat and the echoes of artillery fire became a distant hum. The smoke was somewhat obscured by the sunlight, which was reflected off of the smashed glass that was strewn throughout the city streets. There were isolated pockets of Ukrainian citizens who emerged, their faces marked by terror but also by a determined resolve.

Andriy, who had returned to the battlefield, let his gaze roam over the churned-up dirt and the ruined buildings as he wiped the soot and perspiration from his face. A tree that was tenaciously clinging to its place among the wreckage, a bird flying in the sky above, and a piece of laughter being borne on the wind were some of the traces of life that he noticed despite all of the carnage. It was a jarring reminder that they were battling for much more than simply territory;

rather, they were fighting for the very identity of their nation.

Laura would spend her evenings on the other side of the planet at her office in Virginia, going through an ever-increasing mound of intelligence. Her eyes were reflecting the scrolling lines of code while the gentle illumination from her monitors created harsh shadows across her face. There was a change in Russia's tactics, a subtle shift that showed a deeper and more hidden plan was at play in this situation. She was compelled to investigate the vast amount of material further since the sensation tore at her.

Vitaly gathered with other members of the resistance movement deep within the territory of Belarus. They were hiding out inside of an abandoned barn, where they were perusing maps while seated around an old wooden table. Their information gathering network was represented by a tangled web of blue lines, and it reached all the way from Minsk to Kyiv. As Vitaly relayed the facts that he had gathered, the expressions on their faces hardened with determination. His comments were more than just cautionary tales; they were a rallying cry.

In the meantime, back in Russia, General Kuznetsov was confronted with a challenging mission. His superiors refused to budge, and the morale of his men continued to plummet with each new news of casualties. His troops, though, grumbled. While he was sitting in the frigid, sterile room that functioned as his office, he felt a chill that was not caused by the harsh weather in Russia. It was the cold of uncertainty, the creeping doubt that questioned whether or not they were on the right route that caused them to wonder whether or not they were on the right path.

There was a sense of momentum, a churning river that was getting more forceful with each passing day, in this world that was entwined with goals and anxieties. As people all across the world watched and waited, the participants in this theater of conflict realized that the decisions they made next would not only determine their own destinies, but also that of whole nations.

Putin conducted a secret meeting with his most loyal aides in one of the Kremlin's most hidden nooks and crannies. As they discussed the pullout from Kyiv, the tension in the room was apparent and increased throughout the discussion. Putin presided over the meeting from his seat at the head of the table, his expression as icy as the Russian winter outside. He remained silent while his generals detailed the withdrawal, the casualties, and the setbacks suffered at the hands of the Ukrainian army. The rage that was building up in his eyes was sharply at odds with the seemingly calm motion that he was making with his fingers as he touched the rim of the tea cup he was holding.

Back in the front lines, Andriy stood in front of his soldiers while they fought, their faces showing signs of exhaustion. He could see the wear and tear that the conflict had caused, the burden of anxiety and tiredness. But he also recognized a stubbornness and determination in her. He witnessed a people who were prepared to fight for their country and willing to die in order to defend it. He began to speak with a firm voice, a rallying cry that resounded in the hearts of his warriors, igniting their desire to carry out the mission.

During this time, Laura was becoming more and more confidence in her theory as she navigated the confusing network of computers and displays at the CIA headquarters. She tapped out lines of code at a rapid pace, using convoluted algorithms in order to sort through the masses of data. Her thoughts were a flurry of links and patterns, but there was one thing that stayed consistent: the notion that Russia had a covert motivation for their invasion on Ukraine.

Vitaly discovered that he was a far more integral part of the underground movement in the neighboring country of Belarus than he had ever thought. He had progressed from being a solitary wolf to being an indispensable member of a pack. He had not felt this way in a very long time, but when he sent another important piece of information to his comrades in Ukraine, he had a sense of belonging that he had not felt in a very long time. His acts, which were earlier motivated by the need to stay alive, were now inspired by a feeling of responsibility and the common goal of achieving freedom.

In Moscow, General Kuznetsov was pacing back and forth in his office as his thoughts battled with the difficult task that was in front of him. He was aware of the consequences that would arise as a result of Russia's withdrawal from Kyiv. It was a setback to their military strength and a crack in their supposed invincibility, but they still came out on top. It was never a question of whether they would strike back; rather, the question was when and where.

The sounds of combat continued to reverberate throughout the night as the day faded into darkness, like a spooky tune that was being repeated over and over again. However, hidden within its harsh tones was a suggestion of resiliency and the promise of a daybreak that had the capacity to alter the path that the conflict would take. This was not the conclusion, but rather the beginning, the warm-up for a conflict that was still to come.

As the sun sank below the horizon, throwing long shadows over the scarred cityscape of Kyiv, the globe collectively held its breath in preparation for the next stage of the fight. Even though it was a welcome break, the retreat did not mark the end of the story. It was a tactical reorganization, a brief period of seeming calm before the onslaught of the storm would return in all of its ferocity.

Back in Washington, Laura was sitting in her office with the lights turned down low. Her desk was covered with maps and satellite photos. As the midnight oil burnt, shifting shadows played over her resolute face. Her concerns that the Russians had some kind of covert goal had only been heightened by the information that she had acquired. She was going to argue her side of the case the following day. She was well aware that the world was poised on the brink of a cliff, and that it was imperative to comprehend Putin's overall plan in order to prepare for what was to come.

While this was going on, Andriy's voice could be heard throughout the night in the trenches of the Ukrainian army. He was trying to rally his tired troops. They did not allow the brief lull in the fighting to dampen their spirits. The blaze that burnt so brightly in their eyes shed light on the darkness that around them. In the face of the impending storm, Kyiv remained unshakeable, like an unbreakable lighthouse.

Vitaly and his fellow members of the resistance were gathered together in the middle of Belarus, plotting their next moves. His intel had made its way to the Ukrainian intelligence service, which swung the advantage in their favor. A flicker of optimism appeared after what seemed like an interminable absence of it. Despite being the underdogs, being overlooked, and being persecuted, they were making a difference in the world. The battle has barely begun between them.

The echoes of retreating and reorganizing continued to reverberate all the way from the shimmering dusk of the war-torn landscapes to the humming nerve centers of global power. A pause in the story of struggle and triumph, a precipice peering down into the abyss of the unknown, and a world waiting with bated breath for the next wave of the storm. The aftershocks of the conflict have not yet subsided. The entire globe was getting ready for what was going to happen. The scene had been prepared for the chapters that had not yet   been   written.

CHAPTER 6 "TIDES OF RETRIBUTION"

The following day appeared as a harbinger of change, with the faint sunshine creeping over the horizon to illuminate the huge tracts of Ukrainian territory that were being harshly occupied at the time. But there was a distinct change in the air this morning, like a quiet shift, like the first stirrings of retribution.

Andriy stood tall among his men even though they were in the middle of the war zone. His gaze followed the contours of the destroyed houses and the roadways that were riddled with holes. Under the wounds left by the destruction, he sensed a spirit that would not die and an unrelenting will to fight back. The time for defense had long since gone; what was needed now was a cry to reclaim what had been taken from us unjustly. His radio began to make staticky noises, and a voice from the command center said that "Operation Dawn Strike is a go."

After returning to Washington, Laura discovered that her fears were correct. Her diagnosis on the more fundamental goals of the Russian government was recognized, which provided her with a sense of achievement as well as a gloomy satisfaction. Her efforts were critical in delivering the much-need strategic edge that Ukraine required. However, there was also a personal cost. Her commitment to working long hours and her unrelenting search for the truth had begun to alienate her from the people she cared about. Her small daughter had begun to wonder why her mother was "always busy with her maps." This win left a sour taste in my mouth.

As Vitaly continued to fight alongside the Belarusian resistance, he became increasingly aware of the gravity of the conflict. However, this essential aid to Ukrainian forces did not come without a cost. As a result, his oppressors were struck a terrible blow as a result. His true identity is unknown at this time. He was now on the run from the secret police, who had identified him as a traitor. His picture was plastered all over the city on wanted posters, each of which offered a reward for his safe return. Vitaly, despite the fact that he was being relentlessly pursued, was experiencing an odd wave of exhilaration. He was the one who was going to change everything. He was a spoke in the wheel of transformation, a specter that tormented those in power. He would proceed with his work.

The day devolved into an artillery and gun battle that continued into the night. The Ukrainian army pushed back, forcing the invaders from their homes and cities. This was made possible by new intelligence as well as the stubborn determination of the Ukrainian people. Tanks rumbled over the plains, breaking up the ice-covered terrain with their treads as they traveled. The sky was filled with the roar of fighter planes, and their shadows raced over the ground like lethal and quick apex predators.

Cities that had been tightly held by the invaders for a long time were gradually but steadily opened up for exploration. The Ukrainian people gradually recaptured their motherland by retaking it one square centimeter at a time, one street at a time, and one structure at a time. As Ukrainian flags were raised for the second time, the deafening cheer of their people could be heard reverberating across the wreckage.

Andriy, who was in the thick of the battle, could feel the momentum shifting. He had successfully guided his troops through the arduous conflict in order to secure their first significant win, which was the capture of an important town. However, the win came at a cost. Friendships were severed with those who had been on his side from the beginning of the struggle onward. He wore their dog tags, and the remembrance of them was engraved deeply into his heart, which fueled his determination. Their ultimate efforts would not have been in vain.

The tides of vengeance had begun to turn, and they were cutting deep lines not only on the map but also in the hearts of men and women and in the annals of history.

As the day's fighting progressed, it became a symphony of mayhem and resiliency. Every successful offensive pushed the Ukrainians closer to their goal, and every life lost was a tragedy to be grieved as a harsh consequence of the conflict. Nevertheless, despite the loud echoes of gunfire and the sound of the oncoming tanks, there was an overwhelming feeling of grim satisfaction. They fought back, reclaiming what rightfully belonged to them in the process.

At the headquarters of the CIA, Laura sat with her eyes fixed on the displays that displayed the live satellite feeds. She watched as what appeared to be green blips traveled over the landscape, which she later learned were Ukrainian advances. As she followed the shifting front lines of the fight and monitored the progress of the counteroffensive, her heart raced. However, this triumph was by no means a complete one. As she browsed through the casualty reports, the icy figures that appeared on the screen represented the lives that had been lost. This dreadful truth slowly dawned on her. The human toll that her analysis and subsequent success exacted was glaringly obvious.

During this time, Vitaly found himself in the middle of an increasing whirlwind of activity inside the resistance. They had heard of the triumph of the Ukraine, which boosted their spirits and strengthened their resolve. The invading forces were already under a great deal of stress, and the resistance was getting ready to launch an attack on them with the hopes of piling on even more of it. Vitaly had unexpectedly discovered himself to be an indispensable component of their plans. Despite the risk of having his true identity revealed, he was their most successful scout due to his capacity to move stealthily and pass unobserved through the environment.

Andriy was located on the roof of a structure that was in the process of collapsing in the retaken town. He had his binoculars pointed on the fleeing enemies. His chest hammered with a mixture of relief and grief as his heart raced in his chest. His eyes wandered over to the impromptu graveyard that had been established nearby, the sharp contrast of the white crosses against the snow. on spite of everything, he could still see glimmers of optimism on the faces of his troops and the people who had been saved from the town. He was overcome with an unusual sensation of pride, as well as a sense of oneness and purpose that was stronger than anything he had felt or known before.

As darkness fell, the regions, which bore the profound wounds of the day's fighting, fell into a peaceful hush. The waves of revenge receded for a brief period of time, giving the bruised but unbreakable spirit of the Ukrainian people a brief moment of relief. Every success moved them one step closer to achieving their goal of independence, while every defeat served as a jarring reminder of the cost, they were ready to incur.

In the hushed halls of power, choices were taken and plans were devised for the next day. A squad of freedom fighters were getting ready for their most audacious expedition to yet in a secret base in Belarus. And in one of the towns that had been taken back, a Ukrainian commander was seen kneeling beside the grave of a dead colleague and making a vow to continue the battle.

The day had been lengthy and eventful, with both successes and defeats taking place. However, when the sun set and the night sky took over, it became abundantly evident that this was only the beginning. Even though the tide had shifted, the waves had not yet started to smash on the coast. The conflict was in no way resolved. The repercussions of vengeance would be felt throughout the land, determining the course of events for its inhabitants.

The delicate glow of morning revealed nothing but the harsh light of truth, which exposed the devastation that had been left behind by the conflict. There was no peace to be found in its gentle radiance. The land beneath their feet was scarred and pitted, having been gouged deeply by the machinery of war. The air was filled with the pungent odor of gunpowder and burnt rubber, and the ground was covered with both of these odors.

The tenacious leader Andriy was certain that the daybreak would not provide any alleviation to the situation. Instead, it let him see things more clearly, giving him a sobering perspective on the losses he had experienced and the people who would no longer be there to meet him in the morning. Each defeat tore a hole in the morale of his army's fighting force, but they refused to allow it to deteriorate further. The victory did not come without a price, but it was a price that they were ready to pay. Their determination was as strong as iron; it may flex and strain in the heat of the conflict, but it would not shatter.

While all was going on, Laura was back at the CIA headquarters watching as satellite photographs presented the harsh truth of what had happened. She cried in her heart for the deceased soldiers, individuals she had never met but whose fate was related to her acts, to the information she discovered and sent along. Their fate was tied to her actions, to the information she discovered and passed along. Despite this, she maintained a stony expression on her face as she drew the shifting lines on the map, her mind constantly calculating and always plotting the next move.

In the Belarusian woods at the same time, Vitaly was making his way through the underbrush. He was like a ghost in the woods, a shadow that moved gracefully between the gaps between the trees. He was well aware of the risks that were associated with his employment, including the possibility of being apprehended or perhaps worse. However, the surge of adrenaline and the pressing nature of the situation provided him with an intensified feeling of purpose.

He persisted in his mission in spite of the risks, successfully evading hostile patrols and monitoring. He was an essential cog in the machine, a vital information conduit that was passed along to the Ukrainian armed forces. He was aware of the burden that was being placed on his shoulders as a result of the obligation, which was paradoxically both crushing and invigorating. Each time they were able to sneak past their pursuers unnoticed and avoid capture was a victory in and of itself. But there were other failures and near misses that left him with a racing heart and a sense of dread.

The cost of the conflict continued to mount with each passing hour of the day. But so did the defenders' dogged perseverance, which kept their spirits from breaking despite the overwhelming odds. They battled for every square foot of their land, the embers of vengeance kindling inside their hearts as they did so. They were the waves that carried the conflict onward, and each new wave was a demonstration of their unbreakable determination. And even when darkness fell and the noise on the battlefield subsided, they did not waiver in their determination. In the still of the night, the echoes of their vengeance resounded, serving as a chilling reminder of the wars that had been fought and the conflicts that were still to be waged.

Andriy was able to perceive a pivotal moment in the conflict when the tide of the fight switched and the Ukrainian forces pushed their advantage. A glimmer of light appeared on the horizon for the first time since the beginning of the fight, and those he commanded, both men and women, took heart in this development. His radio sputtered with encouraging reports from the front: territory had been retaken, lives had been spared, and triumphs had been won.

A map of Ukraine was stretched out on the table of the command center's war room, with clusters of color-coded pins marking the shifting battlefield. Each green pin represented a town or city that had been retaken. Andriy contributed one more to the city of Horlivka, which had been oppressed by occupation for a long time but was now finally free.

Back in Washington, Laura was transfixed on the displays in front of her, which displayed maps and feeds that provided her with a real-time perspective of the conflict. Each step that the Ukrainian soldiers took forward was highlighted, and the regions changed from red to blue as they moved forward. But the victories on the field were not the only thing that caught her attention. She was trying to identify any recurring themes or alterations in the enemy's strategy. Her intuitive sense gave her the impression that they were only in the calm before the storm at this point.

In Belarus, Vitaly was not only physically but also emotionally exhausted. He was running on empty. The days and nights had started to run together for him, and the adrenaline that used to stream through his veins had been replaced with an overwhelming sense of fatigue. However, he was aware that he could not afford to relax, especially given the importance of his intelligence to the Ukrainian army. However, the wins were also taking their toll, with each one making the adversary more desperate and hence more deadly. The idea that each of his steps may be his final one kept him awake and cautious at all times.

Despite the victories, there was still a long way to go until the war was done. Every city that was freed and every war that was won just brought about another difficulty and another conflict. It was an exhausting, never-ending cycle of assault and defense, pushing and pulling in all directions. Nevertheless, a more profound comprehension developed in the midst of both the losses and the benefits. It became clear that this conflict was not just fought over territory; rather, it was a struggle for independence and the fundamental essence of a nation.

It seemed as if a deadly determination had settled upon the war-torn countryside as the howling winds swept through it, taking with them the stories of vengeance. Every life that was lost and every bullet that was fired was a monument to the determination of people who were protecting their motherland. The night began to draw its heavy curtain over the land, and with it came the echoes of conflict, a never-ending song of defiance and persistence.

The sun had just begun to rise when it began to paint the sky in various shades of pink and orange. In Kyiv, buildings blasted with bullet holes stood in sharp contrast to the lovely morning. These structures served as a moving reminder of the conflict that was raging for control of the city's core. Here, in the middle of the wreckage, signs of life had started to emerge anew.

Andriy looked like he was exhausted, but he was determined not to let it show on his face as he observed his surroundings. The sour aftertaste of conflict was engraved onto every stone, and every bullet hole bore witness to its presence. Nevertheless, underlying that, he was able to sense a pulse, a beat of resistance and stubbornness. He gazed out at his warriors, and he saw the same resolute look on their faces as was on his. They were prepared for anything that could come their way.

Laura was stationed in the United States at the nerve center of the CIA, where displays were constantly flashing with data and updates. Her attention was drawn to a swift change in Russian movement that occurred suddenly. In a dramatic departure from their prior strategies, they have begun to amass soldiers close to the Crimean Peninsula. Her hunches told her something was not quite right. This was no ordinary regrouping; rather, it was a prelude to something far more terrible that was to come. Her fingers were flying over the keyboard as she hurriedly communicated her findings to her bosses, and she conveyed a feeling of urgency in her delivery.

In the meantime, Vitaly was back on the move in Belarus, this time making his way through the thick woodland when it was still dark. A member of the resistance had informed him of a covert Russian supply channel, which was a possible Achilles heel for the Russians if the Ukrainians were able to exploit it. Despite the potential for harm, the knowledge was of too great a value to pass up.

As Vitaly proceeded farther into area controlled by the adversary, he became aware of a cold hand grasping his heart. The failure would have very serious repercussions. However, he did not face this battle by himself. Back in Kyiv, Andriy was getting his troops ready for another assault on the enemy stronghold. In Washington, Laura was working on a puzzle that she hoped would shed light on the next move that Russia would make.

These were the ebb and flow of revenge, rife with unpredictability and peril, but also with promise and opportunity. Every single step forward was earned by arduous labor, and every single setback served as the impetus for a redoubled effort. The reverberations of the conflict could be felt not only on the battlefield, but also in the hearts and minds of those who dared to disobey authority. The echoes of the war were getting louder.

The courage and determination with which Andriy's soldiers advanced was inspired by the example set by their commander. They were successful in driving the invaders out of Kyiv, and their attention was now focused on Donetsk. Because it was their home, their city, and their nation, they were prepared to battle tooth and nail to protect it. Everyone, men and women alike, braced themselves for the oncoming attack by standing shoulder to shoulder with one another. This was not about winning or being heroic on a personal level; rather, it was about recovering what was legitimately theirs.

In the meantime, Laura's investigation led her down a path that was littered with secret papers and encrypted communications. Her premonition had been correct; Russia was plotting a new onslaught, one that had the potential to change the course of the war. However, the specifics remained obscured by a complex web of confidentiality. She required additional information, preferably anything specific that would give them an advantage over their opponents. She persevered despite her frustration by delving farther into the intelligence matrix, adamant that she would not give up.

On the other side, Vitaly was located deep within the territory of the adversary. He had been successful in infiltrating the supply channel with the help of the cover of the night, but the greater difficulty was still to come. He had to avoid being discovered, obtain information, and then flee without leaving a trail. His extremely risky assignment was made even more difficult by the fact that he was responsible for the lives of a large number of other soldiers.

In the midst of Vitaly's stealthy movement through the darkness, he was startled by a startling noise that sounded like the distant thud of heavy equipment. He stepped closer to the sound, putting himself in danger, and what he saw left him unable to catch his breath. He had never seen anything like the armament that the Russian military were putting together. Vitaly was aware that he needed to communicate this knowledge to Andriy as soon as possible.

The echoes of conflict were becoming increasingly prominent within the beating heart of the resistance. The victories were being recorded in the annals of history, and the taste of freedom was becoming more and more palatable. Every morning offered fresh optimism, while every evening provided a sobering reminder of the tough trip that lay ahead. They needed to prevail in this conflict not just for the sake of their own children and grandchildren, but also for the sake of future generations. The tides of vengeance were beginning to change, and the reverberations were being felt far and wide.

In the midst of the night, Vitaly's breathing grew shallow, and the buzz of the machinery that was all about him was drowned out by the sound of his heartbeat. He was aware that he needed to maintain his composure and keep focused, but the gravity of the situation was slowly dawning on him. His hands were shaking as he used his hidden camera to record as much as he could while praying that no one would spot him. It was quite apparent what his goal was: get the intelligence back to the Ukrainian lines without being discovered.

When Laura got back to her apartment in the middle of Washington, District of Columbia, she found that her corkboard had become covered with a collage of images and maps. Her eyes were red from a combination of tiredness and resolve. Even though it was far past midnight, she did not go to bed since she considered sleep a luxury she could not afford. After what seemed like a decade of reading between the lines and deciphering secret signals, she was finally successful in locating a piece of intelligence that had the potential to alter the path that the battle would take. It was going to be a high-stakes operation that the Russian forces had planned, an assault that was going to be so deadly that it may wipe out the Ukrainian defenses.

During this time, Andriy could feel his heart pounding in his chest as his forces prepared to move into position on the outskirts of Donetsk. The light of morning gradually made its way through the indigo darkness, and when it did so, it created long shadows across the cratered battlefield. The people he was fighting for - his family, his teammates, and his nation – were constantly running through his head as he went into battle. Every new face he saw fueled his resolve and stoked the fire that already existed inside him. Because of his unflinching determination, his men were able to maintain their composure and remain unshaken as they prepared to face the challenges of the day.

The book of retribution had begun, and its pages were filled with accounts of bravery, self-sacrifice, and unwavering determination. Each moment was a demonstration of the resilience of the human spirit, and each win was a ray of light in the midst of the storm. But the conflict was far from done, and as the sun rose higher in the sky and put its golden color on the ravaged battlefield, the protagonists prepared themselves for what was to come in the future.

Vitaly was riding in a stealth helicopter when he got a good look at the devastated countryside that was passing below him. It was like putting together a jigsaw puzzle of burnt buildings, vacant streets, and spectral outlines of towns that were once teeming with activity. His objective had been accomplished, and the information in question was now in the possession of the Ukrainian intelligence. Despite this, the price of triumph weighed heavily on his spirit, with each view of the destruction serving as a jarring reminder of what they had been battling against. He clenched the worn image of his family tightly in his hand and made a solemn commitment to make the next day better for them.

When Laura got back to her workplace, she sat down in front of a plethora of displays, and a gentle glow illuminated her face. She had just gotten off the phone with the director of the CIA, in which she had shared the vital information that she had discovered. The buzzing of her confidential phone, which was a call from the highest levels of authority, broke the stillness that had been present in the room. Her finding was leading to action, and soon, it will resound on the battlefields of Ukraine. Her discovery was leading to action.

At the epicenter of the battle, the early morning stillness in Donetsk was broken by the sound of marching boots and the impassioned whispering of the Ukrainian national song. Andriy took the initiative to stand on the front line and direct the counterattack. His heart was pounding in his chest, and his palm was clenching more tightly on the worn handle of his gun. The sight of the city, which had been damaged but was still standing tall, filled him with an unexplainable sensation that was a mixture of sadness, pride, and an unyielding determination. At the break of dawn on the new day, the first indications of their retribution and the beginnings of their reclaiming appeared.

The echoes of their footfall signaled a pivotal moment in the conflict as they unfolded alongside the chapter of revenge. The heroes, despite being dispersed in different parts of the world, were unwittingly cooperating with one another and their activities were intertwined in the intricate web of the struggle. The tides of battle were changing, but there was still a long way to go before victory was assured. Their battles were witnessed by the sun, which was a flaming ball in the sky, and it threw long, intimidating shadows on the ground below them. They marched on, motivated by the hope of a better future, which was a future for which they were prepared to fight, despite the fact that the odds were stacked against them.

As the sun continued to climb higher in the sky, Vitaly's chopper landed in a safe area that served as a temporary military station. He entered the building, his boots making a crunching sound on the gravel. The atmosphere was thick with a smell that was a combination of gasoline, perspiration, and the underlying, pervasive odor of terror. At the very least for the time being, Vitaly was aware that he was back in his own house. The faces of the soldiers, who were dressed in Ukrainian uniforms, were etched with expectation as they surged towards him. Because of his brilliance, he had become a very valuable asset, and his reputation continued to grow despite the fact that communication had broken down.

When Laura returned to Washington, she was met with a great deal of opposition from her superiors. Her results indicated to a possible covert operation by Russia, a stratagem concealed deep within the folds of the invasion. Her findings pointed to a possible covert operation by Russia. However, without undeniable proof, putting this plan into effect would be fraught with danger. However, despite the fact that her views were regarded with skepticism, she would not back down. She made the decision to take action on her own accord after years of feeling powerless and harboring a firm belief that she was right. She had spent a number of hours engaged in careful preparation before getting ready to go on a secret operation to confirm her findings.

Andriy commanded his troops as they traversed the rubble-strewn streets of Donetsk in the middle of the fighting. His heart was thumping against his ribcage, and each of those beats was an ode to defiance. They were outgunned and outnumbered, but they had the benefit of being in their own territory. Andriy was not in the path of the bullet, but it nevertheless managed to hit the wall behind him. It was a sobering reminder of the terrible fact, which was that moving on was like dancing with one's own mortality. However, as he turned around to gaze at the faces of his fellow soldiers, he saw resolve that had been honed by desperation. They continued forth, propelled ahead by the love they had for the city.

On both sides of the conflict, victories and defeats were tallied, and the tide of the fight shifted back and forth like a turbulent sea. Every day provided its own unique set of obstacles and opportunity. The personal conflicts that our main characters had to overcome served as a microcosm for the conflict as a whole. It was a battle for one's very existence, for one's independence, and for a future in which peace would prevail. Each choice, each triumph, and each defeat helped to fan the fires of resolution in their souls, therefore shaping them into the warriors they needed to be. As the day drew to a close, the harsh truth of battle became abundantly obvious.

The capital city of Kyiv witnessed a revival of the Ukrainian troops' forward impetus. They had been successful in stopping a Russian supply convoy that was moving toward the city's core, which swung the momentum of the conflict in their favor. They followed the leads that Vitaly had supplied for them based on the intelligence he had gleaned from his extensive network of sources. In spite of his personal exhaustion and the emotional toll that his double life had on him, he experienced a surge of vindication when the word that the operation had been successful reached him. However, he was well aware that there was no room for self-satisfaction because the conflict was by no means done.

The path that Laura had traveled had led her to Poland, where she was currently operating under the guise of a diplomatic ambassador. She began her research in the middle of Warsaw by gathering information, conducting data analysis, and cross-checking her results. She was aware of a clock in the back of her head that was ticking. Each minute was a potential life that might be saved or lost, and each second was a priceless commodity. Sleep had become a luxury for her, and although though eating was a need, she often forgot to eat. She felt that her burning drive to uncover the genuine objectives of Russia supported her and provided her with the determination and adrenaline she needed to keep going.

While everything was going on, Andriy and his soldiers continued to advance deeper into Donetsk. Each building they took back and each street they freed seemed like a personal victory to those fighting with them. However, they did not come without a price. His forces were falling in number, his soldiers were worn out, and he was running out of supplies. The images of every deceased comrade, as well as those of every citizen injured in the crossfire, were seared into his consciousness, serving as a constant reminder of the cost of their uprising. Andriy felt the weight of leadership pressing down on him more heavily than it had before among the mayhem and the loss. However, he also experienced a resolute resolve and a dogged drive to defend his city and the people who lived there from the attackers.

Even though the skirmishes were still going on, the story that was being told was one of fortitude and determination. These were stories of individual fortitude and self-sacrifice, tales that mirrored the larger effort of a nation to reclaim its rightful place as the dominant power in its own territory. The dogged determination of the Ukrainian people shined through in each and every conflict, skirmish, victory, and defeat. Every eye on the planet was seeing the dramatic tides of revenge in Ukraine as the next chapter of the conflict proceeded to play out, and the whole world watched in eager expectation.

Tucked up in the shadows of an ancient brick structure, Vitaly rested his back against the wall as the moon cast its gentle light on him. His pulse was thumping in his chest, and he could feel the excitement coursing through his veins. This passageway, which can be found in the middle of Minsk, was a well-known smuggling conduit that the Russians had not yet discovered. He was looking for an individual who, given the appropriate set of circumstances, would sell information to whoever had the greatest offer. He was waiting for this contact. As Vitaly tightened his grasp on the stack of cash in his fingers, he felt a lump begin to develop in the back of his throat.

The sound of gravel crunching suddenly filled the air. At the entrance of the back alleyway, a towering person suddenly emerged. Vitaly was only able to make out the man's outline due to the fact that the man's hat was casting a shadow over his face. It was his connection with them.

While this was going on, the center of Kyiv was on fire, and the city was lit up by the brightness of the blazing barricades. The background was always filled with the piercing whine of approaching artillery, with the odd earth-shaking explosion serving as a punctuation mark. Andriy moved with a level head and a dogged drive despite the pandemonium. It was a symbolic triumph that had boosted their morale when they had retaken their former neighborhood, which they had done with their men. But there was still a long way to go in this conflict.

Andriy's attention was drawn to a once-familiar structure that had been damaged by fire and was now partially collapsed. It was his former place of education. He recalled how, as a little child, he used to run down those corridors, and the sound of laughing would reverberate off the walls. Now, it served as a sobering reminder of how much this battle had cost.

Laura was bent over her workstation in Warsaw, Poland, with the brightness of her computer screen illuminating her determined face. She was halfway across the world. She had just gotten evidence that backed up her assumptions, which were that Russia was covering something up. The situation was far more dire than she had anticipated. After some reflection, she realized that the Russian invasion was about more than just territory or political power. It all came down to resources, namely one that had the potential to shift the power dynamic on a global scale. She felt shivers run down her spine at the disclosure.

She was aware that it was her duty to alert her superiors and reveal Russia's actual intentions to the rest of the world. However, she was also aware that the risk to her life was currently greater than it had ever been. Despite this, Laura was unable to deny the fire of self-determination that was igniting inside her. She had moved one step closer to uncovering the truth, and Ukraine had moved one step closer to receiving justice.

In Minsk, Vitaly's contact, who was hidden in the darkness of the night, slipped a tattered and worn-out envelope over the icy concrete. As Vitaly snatched it up, his heart hammered in his chest. His fingertips lightly brushed across the rough roughness as he did so. There was important information and information regarding the movements of Russian forces along the border inside.

"Are these details correct?" Vitaly growled, and his eyes did not wander from the man standing in front of him.

The man answered with a hint of venom in his voice as he slipped the wad of cash that Vitaly had gave him into his pocket. "As accurate as your money," the man said.

Vitaly could feel the burden of the knowledge he was holding in his hands as the shadowy figure disappeared into the night. This was no longer simply about Belarus; the stakes had significantly increased at this point. It was imperative that he communicate this knowledge to the Ukrainians.

Back downtown Kyiv, Andriy and his men had taken cover in a location that was formerly occupied by a lively bazaar. It had been reduced to little more than a war-torn wreck at this point. However, it belonged to them. They had succeeded in expelling the Russian forces from the area, but they were aware that it was only a matter of time until the Russians attempted to retake it.

Andriy stood there, staring out over the ravaged metropolis, which was littered with the smoldering relics of his past, and he thought of his family, who was currently hiding out in Lviv. The rage that had been dormant within him erupted again. This was his house, and he was willing to do everything it needed to keep it safe for his family.

Laura was putting the pieces together in her workplace in Warsaw at the time. She spent a great deal of time studying the geological surveys, as well as the maps and reports on army movements. Russia wasn't just invading Ukraine; it was also going for certain parts of Ukraine that were recognized for their abundant amounts of a rare mineral that is required for the production of high-tech goods. A paradigm shift in the way the modern world operates.

As she worked on the report, her hands were trembling uncontrollably. She was aware that this was far larger than any of the others. It was possible that it might become a worldwide battle, and they were running out of time to prevent this from happening. She felt a mixture of terror and relief as she pushed the "send" button on her keyboard. There was no turning back now; it was too late. The world will eventually become aware of the truth; it was only a matter of when it would become public knowledge.

The static crackling from the field radio was the only sound that could be heard in the deserted marketplace. Andriy was extremely tense as he waited for the person on the other end of the line to give him the information. The announcement was made that "We have won in Mariupol," and even over the static, the sense of relief was clear. In the middle of the never-ending misery, the misfit band of troops and volunteers broke out into cheers, providing a little respite from the gloom.

Andriy tightened his grip on the weathered map in his hands and began to trace the line of authority back towards Russia. Every day was a battle, and every inch that was restored was a win. However, each win came at a great price. He thought of the young faces that had entered his ranks, full of bravado and national pride, and how those faces had become hardened and tormented by the reality of war. He thought of the young faces that had joined his ranks.

Vitaly, who was stationed in Minsk at the time, was able to decipher a telegram that confirmed his intelligence had been passed on to the Ukrainian soldiers. He let out a breath, not aware that he had been holding it for some time. His chest began to pound with a feeling that was equal parts relief and anxiety. He was in over his head at this point, and officially considered a betrayer to the administration that he had formerly served.

In Warsaw, Laura's disclosure was the spark that ignited a series of events. Her discoveries had been brought to the attention of NATO, and emergency meetings were being organized as a result. While she was watching the news, the significance of her finding became clearer to her as world leaders openly stated their fears over Russia's invasion of Ukraine and the possibly catastrophic repercussions it may have. During this time, she realized that her finding could have a significant impact.

In spite of the stressful environment, Laura experienced a peculiar sense of serenity wash over her. When we understood the goals of our adversary, we gained clarity, and when we gained clarity, we gained the strength to strategize and fight back. She was no longer an observer of this conflict from the outside. She was a part of it, and the information that she gained became a weapon that was just as important as the firearms that the Ukrainian troops had in their hands.

As the globe reacted to the shifting tides, our characters found themselves in the middle of the conflict, with their destinies entwined with that of their countries. Every triumph gave them hope, every setback strengthened their determination, and every day took them one step closer to a confrontation that would alter the course of their lives indefinitely.

Back on the Ukrainian front, Andriy watched as a young soldier, who couldn't have been much older than his own kid, made his way out from under the debris of a structure that had been destroyed in the fighting. The patches on his clothing that identified his regiment were obscured because of the heavy coating of dust that was covering them. Andriy had seen that wild-eyed, distant look on far too many people during the conflict, and it was a sharp reminder of the cruelty of war that the child had.

Andriy stepped closer to him and put a reassuring hand on him as he was shrugging his shoulders. "Son," he began, his tone of voice being kind and reassuring, "you're safe now." But when he peered into the eyes of the young soldier, he realized that his words could not provide any solace for him. His consciousness was elsewhere, and he was unable to break out of the nightmare he was experiencing. It was a frightening reminder of the human cost of these minor successes, a price paid in lost innocence and stolen youth. These were the prices paid for these small victories.

Vitaly, in the meantime, kept up his risky dance with the resistance while it was taking place in the shadowy nooks of Minsk. His function had expanded, and he was no longer only a channel through which information was transmitted; rather, he was turning into an essential cog in the machine. Tonight, he was scheduled to meet with a leader of the opposition who was only identified by the name "Sparrow." Her cover name was a cryptic reference to a hardy little bird that could make it through the hardest of winters, and it was a sign of optimism.

Laura's study, which began with Russia's objective and expanded to include the geopolitical ramifications of this clash, was conducted back in Warsaw. Sanctions and condemnations had been sent all around the world in response to the incident, but behind closed doors, relationships were being evaluated. Even in the room where the study was being done, the tension could be felt. She and her colleagues worked nonstop, and their study wound up becoming an essential component of the overall plan for the worldwide operation.

The story of a dissident working within the Belarusian government who was passing information on to the Ukrainians captivated Laura, and she found herself pulled to it. If they were to improve this relationship, it is possible that they would be able to undermine the partnership that exists between Russia and Belarus. As her curiosity grew, she couldn't help but speculate about the unknown someone on the other end of the line who was acting in the background.

These were the decisive moments in the course of the conflict, the movements that occurred behind the scenes that molded the landscape of the battlefield. Our heroes, in their various positions, were contributing to a turn in the tide, and every move they took sent ripples into the conflict's fabric, forging a new reality that was yet unknown and teetering on the brink of significant change.

A recent Russian retreat was located in the hectic center of Kyiv, and the recovered streets there throbbed with a renewed life after being reclaimed. The decimated structures and scattered bullet holes that marred an otherwise picture-perfect cityscape were visible reminders of the price that this victory exacted. Despite this, the locals radiated determination, and each of them was a living tribute to the tenacity of the Ukrainian people.

Andriy, who was maintaining his composure despite the mayhem, switched his attention to the charred remains of a once-bustling office building. Its windows, which had previously been glittering, were now shattered and desolately open. He had a twinge of regret, but he forced it out of his mind. This was not the time for emotion; steel was what was needed. He rallied his troops and issued directions and directives, making it very apparent to them that their next mission was to keep pushing and regain every inch, street, and city.

Vitaly found himself in the midst of a secret meeting with Sparrow and several other members of the resistance in the quiet shadows of Minsk. The threat posed by these encounters was never far from his mind, causing his heart to pound violently in his chest. The space was softly lit, full of hushed murmurs, and filled with the odd clink of metal; it was a sharp contrast to the bustling core of Kyiv, yet it was as alive in its own way. The course of Belarus's destiny was being charted right here, among these courageous individuals.

Vitaly felt the weight of his job as he relayed the most recent intelligence he had gathered from the Ukrainian battlefield. Each piece of information that he communicated had the potential to save lives and to change the direction that the battle would go. As he took a look around the room at the faces that were carved with resolve, he came to the realization that he was no longer an outsider; rather, he was a participant in the fight and a gear in the wheel of liberation.

Laura was sitting in Warsaw, crouched over her desk, with a mountain of documents and reports spread out before her. Laura was located thousands of kilometers away. Her eyes darted across the page of the paper, which was a record of a phone conversation that had been overheard between two Belarusian officials. The use of coded language and indirect allusions, both of which pointed to the possibility of an insider who was leaking information to the Ukrainians, were two of the indicators. She experienced a flurry of ecstasy throughout her body. It would be a huge step forward if they could locate and safeguard this source of information.

when a result, when the counteroffensives persisted and regained areas, each of our characters dove further into their respective responsibilities. Each triumph, each setback, and each newly discovered piece of intelligence contributed another thread to the complex web of the fight. The tenacity of Andriy, the bravery of Vitaly, and the analytical intellect of Laura — all of these things were pieces on the big chessboard that was this battle, and their next movements had not yet been determined.

Andriy and his troops started on a hazardous mission in the dead of night, under the cover of a faint cover provided by a sliver of the moon. The goal is to retake control of the strategically significant city of Kherson. Their march was broken up by random bursts of gunfire, and the terrible cries of the night played their own macabre symphony in the background.

They arrived at the city's outskirts when it was still dark, and the once lively city was now a desolate silhouette against the vastness of the starry horizon. Suddenly, a flare soared up into the night sky, casting a ghostly glow across the countryside that quickly faded away. It was the indication that they'd been watching for - the opposition in the city was getting ready to rise up.

At the same moment, hundreds of miles away in Minsk, Vitaly was crouched over a homemade radio with headphones pressed firmly against his ears. His heart was beating in time with the crackling static as he waited for a sign, some indication that his knowledge had made a difference in the situation. While he was holding his breath, a scrambled transmission said that "The Falcon has landed." As a wave of relaxation washed over Vitaly, he let out a sigh. His information was taken down and processed. The procedure was successful.

When Andriy and his troops returned to Kherson, they were joined in their assault by members of the local resistance. The sound of the rifles reverberated against the deteriorating structure of the metropolis as firefights broke out across the city like frenzied fireworks. The war was bloody and punishing, but the Ukrainians stood their own because they were motivated by the idea of gaining their freedom.

at the meantime, Laura was at her office, where she was wringing every ounce of her being out in an effort to hear the most recent news from Kherson. The stress was evident as she hung on to every word and every update that was transmitted via her private line. The night stretched on, and eventually she received the news that she had been anticipating: "Kherson is once again under the control of the Ukrainians."

She felt ecstasy coursing through her veins, but there was no time for her to rejoice. She had another paper to review as well as another lead to investigate. The conflict has only just begun. She flashed a brief glimpse at a photograph that was sitting on her desk. It was a straightforward family portrait that had been shot many years earlier. This photograph served as a jarring reminder of what she was fighting for.

The Ukrainians were victors, and when daylight broke, they stood tall among the rubble of Kherson. The price of their victory was written in the wreckage that surrounded them as well as on the faces of the fatigued but resolute warriors. Andriy turned around to survey his troops, and he couldn't help but feel a surge of pride. They were able to pull it off. They had taken back control of their city.

The waves of battle were unrelenting: losses and successes, celebration and misery. And despite this, Andriy, Vitaly, and Laura continued to do their parts in the bigger picture, each in their own unique way. Not only were their personal experiences, sacrifices, and successes influencing the course of their own destiny, but also those of their nations. They still had more battles to fight and more triumphs to earn since the war had not yet come to an end.

A significant victory for the Ukrainian army took place in the city of Mariupol, located in the country's south. They were able to effectively reclaim the city port, a key position that would significantly impede the Russian supply lines once they were in their possession once more. Andriy, who had been in charge of leading the attack, had a surge of joy as he witnessed the Ukrainian flag being raised once more above the harbor.

Nevertheless, even in the middle of all the rejoicing, the sour taste of defeat remained constantly present. A great number of warriors had not survived to witness this triumph. One of them had been a young guy by the name of Roman. He was a valiant soldier who had battled beside Andriy from the very beginning of the fight. Roman had been killed. Andriy had been profoundly affected by the loss of Roman, but it had also served to strengthen his determination. As he stared out over the reclaimed harbor, he realized that his thoughts were as chaotic as the water that was in front of him.

The work that Vitaly had to do in Minsk was becoming more and more hazardous. Despite this, he continued on nevertheless, propelled by a strong feeling of responsibility that much surpassed any anxiety he could have had. He carried out a daring attack on a Belarusian military post in the middle of the night, while it was still dark outside, in order to acquire important intelligence for the Ukrainian troops. As he moved discreetly across the facility, he couldn't help but reflect on the peril he was placing himself in, even though he was well aware that this was a risk that had to be taken. He was able to obtain the information and get away without being discovered, which is a little win but one that might have big ramifications in the future.

During this time, Laura's inquiry was beginning to yield results. All of the subtle hints and the intercepted calls pointed to a person she had begun referring to as "The Raven," and they all pointed to the same person. Whoever or whatever this insider was, they were feeding the Ukrainian soldiers with intelligence that was extremely helpful. Laura felt a sense of relief but was also quite interested. She was aware that she needed to discover the identity of "The Raven" not only to protect them, but also to maybe fortify the connection between them in terms of the knowledge they shared. The stakes were tremendous, and the game was getting progressively more difficult as it progressed.

The waves of revenge were becoming stronger by the day as time went on. Each of our characters, operating inside their respective domain, were able to see these alterations and their effects. Their deeds and decisions shaped both the overall trajectory of the fight as well as their own individual destiny, and their individual triumphs and defeats were intricately woven into this complex tapestry. They were surrounded by the reverberations of war, which served as a jarring reminder of the course of action they had decided to take and the conflict that was still to come.

The pathways taken by the characters begin to diverge even further, and the particular choices made by each character become increasingly significant in the larger, more fluid picture of the battle. Each moment is an intricate component of the maelstrom, and each choice echoes across the turbulent tides of conflict. There are victories and losses, triumphs and sorrows, and each moment is an intricate element of the maelstrom.

Andriy may be seen in the distance in Mariupol, his silhouette cast against the ablaze background of the reclaimed city harbor. A silent and defiant testimony to their hard-earned victory, the Ukrainian flag waves valiantly against the crimson-hued sky as it flutters fiercely in the wind. Even though the lives that were taken hurt him deeply, the seed of hope that was planted in his breast is growing stronger with each passing moment.

Back in Belarus, Vitaly hides in the darkness and watches as daylight approaches, certain that the stolen information is secure in his possession. It had never before seemed so worthy to put his life at danger. The information that he has accumulated is a potent resource that has the potential to alter the course of the conflict. Even though he is just one piece in this complicated game of chess, he is aware that each and every move is significant.

In the meantime, Laura is sitting by herself in her office on the other side of the ocean. The light from her computer screen is forming long shadows in the dimly lit room. The enigmatic communications she receives from "The Raven" lead her farther into a maze that is filled with lies and concealment. Despite this, she does not avoid it because she is aware that solving these puzzles might significantly alter the situation. Her determination is unshakeable, and the ferocity of her pursuit is consistent throughout.

Their experiences are intertwined with those of others involved in a fight that spans many nations and continents. Their individual triumphs and defeats, hopes and concerns are now intertwined with a greater tale, one that is far from being concluded. As the sun goes down on this chapter, the echoes of war continue to resound, serving as a sad reminder of battles fought and won, as well as those that are yet to be fought.

This big and sad show is about to go on to the next act, and the stage and all of the actors are ready. As a result, we look into the unknown future, where our heroes will face new obstacles, achieve new wins, and uncover previously hidden truths. Although they are traveling in different directions, their lives are irrevocably linked together by the unrelenting passage of time and the unstoppable onslaught of conflict.

CHAPTER 7 "SHADOWS OF THE PAST"

1998 is the year in question. A young Andriy is seen accompanying his father on a walk as the two of them create frost with their breath in the bitterly cold weather. Andriy's father, a severe individual who radiated experience and carried the weight of the world on his shoulders, imparted a piece of guidance to his son that he would take with him into adulthood: "Never forget, son, that freedom is the most important thing a man can have. And it is our responsibility to defend it no matter what the cost may be.

Andriy thinks about the things that his father had spoken as he stands in the middle of the wreckage of Mariupol in the current day. His entire life is living proof of the validity of this ideology. As a member of the military, he has vowed to do all in his power to safeguard Ukraine's independence. The recollection of the lessons that he was taught by his father and the affection he has for his country drive his willingness to fight, despite the difficulty of the situation.

While all is going on in the present, we take a trip back in time to Vitaly's youth in the 1990s. He is a bright and inquisitive young man who has grown up under the oppressive rule of Lukashenko's government. When he was just eleven years old, his parents were taken away because they were political dissidents who dared to dream of a freer Belarus. The whispered mutterings of "The Raven" turned into a guiding light, a personification of resistance that encouraged him to take the perilous road of insurrection.

Now that Vitaly is working with the local opposition, the memories of his parents serve as a continuous reminder of the high risks involved. Because of their sacrifices and the hope of seeing Belarus become free, he is compelled to keep playing the risky game of espionage. He is aware that he treads a fine line, but the specter of his parent's hopes and "The Raven's" mysterious motivation steer him in the right direction.

In Washington, D.C., we go back in time to when Laura was just starting out at the CIA as a new employee. She had always been intrigued by the challenge of solving mysteries and the excitement of unearthing previously concealed information. This curiosity was the impetus behind her decision to pursue a certain line of work. But in addition to that, there was a personal justification. A number of years ago, her elder brother, who was a journalist who investigated mysteries, went missing in Russia while pursuing a clue. His last communication to her had been: "Dig deeper, Laura. There is more going on than meets the eye.

Now that Laura is investigating the mysteries surrounding the conflict, she is compelled by an unquenchable desire to learn the truth about what happened. She is no longer merely an analyst for the CIA; rather, she is a woman on a mission, searching for solutions not only for her nation but also for her brother. As the light from the screen shines on her face in the dim room, she solemnly resolves in her mind that she will not overlook any possibility.

Each character's history has had a role in shaping who they are today, placing them at the frontline of a battle that is far greater than themselves. Their drive to play their part in this expansive narrative is fueled by their reasons, which are wrapped up in their personal histories and past hurts. Their histories interweave to create a pattern of resiliency and defiance, which is colored by the memories of their pasts and how they have shaped their present.

We take a look back at Andriy's early days of training in the Ukrainian military as we travel through his history. He confronted the arduous difficulties of training, which included the frigid nights and the sweltering days, with a fresh face and equipped with the wisdom that he had learned from his father. The recollection of his first genuine test of perseverance comes to the surface: he was required to maintain a defensive line against training artillery for twenty-four exhausting hours. On that night, he realized the full extent of the responsibility that came with the freedom that his father had been talking about. It was a weight that he decided to shoulder, despite the fact that it was difficult, unpleasant, and sometimes unappreciated.

Andriy reaches up and caresses the dog tag that is strung around his neck as he walks through the bombed-out streets of Mariupol.

The reminder of his history strengthens his determination. As he surveys his troops, he hears his father's voice in his head, saying, "Freedom is the most valuable thing a man can own. And it is our responsibility to defend it no matter what the cost may be.

Vitaly's recollections in Belarus go all the way back to the meetings of the underground resistance that he attended when he was younger. There, he made the acquaintance of Alena, a ferocious lady whose words fueled the fires of his determination. Alena, who would go on to become his wife and the mother of his kid after some time had passed. Alena, who had the courage to speak out against Lukashenko's tyranny, was taken away because of her bravery.

Now, in the faint light of a concealed bunker, Vitaly traces the weathered image of his wife and kid with his fingertips. He is aware of the potential downsides, as well as the potential cost. However, the recollection of Alena's stubbornness and the necessity of providing a better future for his kid motivate him to continue. It's possible that the mutterings of "The Raven" prompted him to start along this path, but the deaths of his loved ones have made the fight for freedom an even greater need.

We are transported to Laura's past as we arrive in Washington, District of Columbia. Now that she is back in school, her brother Mark is introducing her to a world full of mysteries that haven't been solved and stories that haven't been told. Mark, who vanished while working on a piece about political conspiracies, and left Laura with just a cryptic letter that said, "Dig deeper, Laura." There is more going on than meets the eye.

In the here and now, Laura continues to go forward with her inquiry using the analytical abilities she has acquired along with an insatiable need for the truth. The image of her brother, who is never far from her thoughts, gives her the drive to unravel the mysteries of this conflict and unearth the realities that lie buried behind the lies and fabrications that have been spread about them. Her own mission and her professional obligation have come together to forge an unshakeable determination in her.

As time goes on, the events of their past continue to reverberate in the choices they make now, shaping the ways in which they navigate this more complicated battlefield. Their experiences have molded them, their tragedies have hardened them, and their determination, which was forged in the gloom of their pasts, now propels them towards a future that is fraught with unpredictability.

In the calm of her study in Washington, DC, Linda flipped through some old photographs of her family. She halted in front of a picture of her father, who appeared to be a serious guy and had a military cut. Her father was a soldier of the Cold War, but she didn't hear much of him talking about his experiences. Instead, he immersed himself in his profession, and the weight of the secrets he harbored appeared to be bearing down on him as the years passed. However, she recalled how his eyes lighted up every time she solved a challenging problem, and how he gradually encouraged her towards a life that was committed to knowledge and service. Her resilience in the face of hardship was thanks in large part to the unspoken and ever-present presence of the past. She became an extraordinary analyzer as a result of both his training and her intense passion for solving mysteries.

During this time, Anton was sitting in his secure residence in the middle of Minsk, looking through maps. The only light in the room came from the candles, which gave off a smoky glow. He planned probable routes, safe places, and areas of interest with great care, since his life was now completely occupied with the fight for liberation. His history served as a continual reminder of the reasons he was fighting. His parents, both of whom suffered political persecution at the hands of Lukashenko's administration, served as a guiding light for him. Because of their sacrifice, he had an insatiable want to see the independence of his nation realized. He had trouble remembering them, and the sorrow was always there with him; yet, he used it as motivation. During the most difficult parts of his ordeal, he forced himself to keep going by seeing their faces.

In Kyiv, Sofia braced herself against a deteriorating wall with her sniper weapon resting in her lap. She was filthy all over, and the blue in her eyes seemed worn out. On the other hand, there was a ferocious resolve there. She had been a youngster when the Orange Revolution took place, and during that time, she had seen both the optimism and the disappointment in the eyes of the people. She was familiar with the face of corruption and the ramifications of a government that was distant from the people it served. It was these recollections that drove her to safeguard her country and her people in the present day. The gun that she held in her hands was not just a weapon, but also a tool to mold a more favorable future.

In these still moments, as they addressed their history and girded themselves for the future, they were more than simply a CIA analyst, a freedom fighter, or a soldier. They were representations of defiance and of optimism. They were the epitome of the fight against tyranny and injustice. Their history was not only a shadow; rather, it was a flame, a guiding light that would take them through the most difficult conflicts that were still to come.

Linda ran her finger over the creased image of her father dressed in his military uniform while she was working in her study. When she was a small kid, she recalled that he would take her to the Lincoln Memorial. She had fond memories of such trips. He would comment as he looked up at the monument of Abraham Lincoln, "People like him and us, we're the watchdogs of freedom. Always be on the lookout." His words rang in her head. She now realized that the conflicts he fought were not simply with external foes, but also with the demons that were within him. Linda's determination stiffened. Not only was it important to her to keep the principles that her father had taught in her, but it was also important to make sure that the struggles that her father had endured would not be in vain.

Back in Belarus, Anton's train of thought was broken when there was a quiet knock on the door. It was Olga, another person involved in the resistance movement. She presented a tattered and worn-out notepad to me. "I found it," she announced. It was the journal that his mother kept. By reading her remarks, he was taken back to a period in his life when things were less complicated. The words penned by his mother, which were packed with such optimism for a more liberated Belarus, instilled in him a rekindled sense of purpose. He understood the purpose of his struggle; it was to fulfill the goal that both of his parents had shared with him, a desire that he was now obligated to make a reality.

While in Kyiv, Sofia's mind began to wander back to when she was much younger. Her mother would cuddle her into bed at night while telling her stories of brave Cossack warriors. These tales would put the seed of resiliency and bravery in her heart. Her father, a poor school teacher, instilled in her a desire to fight for a society in which children might grow up hearing stories of love rather than stories of violence. He was the one who showed her the beauty of the world beyond weapons and battle. Every shot she fired and every foe she defeated was for the sake of the promise that was contained in that universe. She had made a promise that she was going to honor, regardless of the consequences.

As Linda, Anton, and Sofia navigated their way through the maze of their memories, not only did they come face to face with their histories, but they also saw a peek of the future that they were working so hard to construct for themselves. They were aware that the way ahead was fraught with danger and that the odds were stacked against them. Despite this, they remained steadfast in their determination. Because inside the reverberations of their history, they discovered the symphony of their bravery, a courage that was going to be the one to create the future.

Linda stayed there in her study where she continued to go through the items that belonged to her father. She unearthed a secret note that her father had penned during the time of the Cold War, which was hidden among the mounds of medals, letters, and old black-and-white photographs. She was able to decipher it without much difficulty since he had taught her the cipher when she was a little girl as a delightful game to play on gloomy days. When she found out about it, she felt a chill down her spine. It was a prophesy of Russian goals for Europe, and the events that are taking place in Ukraine hauntingly resound with those objectives. She saw that this confrontation was not a random act of hostility but rather the culmination of an earlier plot, and she also realized that the past was spilling into the present at this point.

While in Belarus, Anton treasured the comfort that his mother's notebook brought him by keeping it near at hand. He opened the book at random, and one of the pages fell open to a sentence that his mother had written on the day he was born. She shared with him her hopes and aspirations for his future: fantasies of a life liberated from tyranny and oppression, thoughts of his upbringing in a nation where the atmosphere was permeated with liberty rather than fear. Although she had not survived to see that day, the things that she had spoken had inspired a fiery passion inside him. He would do all in his power to ensure that his mother's hopes and ambitions were not relegated to the status of faded words on an old paper.

In the middle of Kyiv, Sofia went back to her childhood house, which was now nothing more than a broken shell beneath a gray sky. The shelling had removed the wallpaper that she and her father had hung together, exposing the hard bricks that were underneath. An antique chessboard, a relic from the numerous hours spent plotting and laughing with her father over a game of chess, was discovered by her here, in the middle of the wreckage and rubbish. She couldn't help but grin as she thought back to his words: "In chess, as in war, you have to anticipate your opponent's moves." After some reflection, Sofia understood that this conflict was not only one of weapons and tanks, but also of brains and tactics.

Their histories were not just chapters in their life stories; rather, they constituted the fundamental foundation of the war they were currently engaged in. At the same time that Linda was unearthing secrets from the past, Anton discovered motivation in a dream, and Sofia developed a plan while playing a game. The ghosts of their history were shaping them and getting them ready for the ordeals that were ahead. However, despite the weight of these shadows, they discovered an unparalleled strength inside them. It was the strength that came from their history, the power that came from their beliefs, and the strength that they would bring with them into the thick of the conflict.

As the chapter progresses, the focus shifts from the personal to the professional, reflecting the changes that have occurred in the lives of our protagonists. As for Linda, she discovered that she had to struggle with the prophesy that her father had given, putting the pieces of the past together, and attempting to identify the links with the present. While toiling away well into the night in her office in Langley, she painstakingly spread-out maps of Eastern Europe, methodically noting key areas and drew lines indicating possible routes of advancement. Her coworkers stared at her as if she had lost her mind, but she saw something that they did not; she saw a ghost from the past that was haunting the present.

As she decoded her father's prognosis from the 1970s on Russia's imperialistic aspirations, she felt a chill go up the back of her neck. The deciphered communication exposed a comprehensive strategy for invasions into Eastern Europe, with Ukraine serving as a pivotal point in the operation. Was this invasion only the first step towards a more massive assault? The mere notion of that sent shivers down her spine. She devoted herself even more fully to her task, resolute to discover as much information as she could about the impending danger.

During this time, Anton found himself becoming more and more involved in the intricate workings of the resistance movement in Belarus. In the midst of all the chaos, he turned to his mother's notebook and her aspirations for freedom as his guide to morality. The dreams that his mother had written down all those years ago were more than simply visions of a brighter future; they were a call to action to make those dreams come true. Anton realized that he was more than simply a member of the resistance; he was also a custodian of the ideal that his mother had for their family.

Back in Kyiv, the strategy that Sofia had learnt while playing chess was being used into the preparation of their defenses at this point. She devised various attack paths, located weaknesses, and suggested counteroffensives in her plan. Her time spent playing chess with her father was not wasted time; rather, it served as preparation for situations precisely like this one.

In spite of the fact that they were fighting separate conflicts, they were bound together by a shared enemy: the past. Their respective histories served to inspire them, provide direction for them, and bolster them. Their histories were the invisible forces that guided them towards a future of unknown destiny as they struggled to come to terms with the roles they were playing in the current fight.

As Linda struggled to make sense of the intricate geopolitical conundrum, she found that her thoughts kept coming back to the same question: why Ukraine? The questions that her mother asked her father's notes did not have a clear response, but the numerous circles and lines that were drawn around Ukraine's location on the map appeared to shout its significance. She continued to scour classified files, historical archives, and intelligence snippets, looking for anything that would offer a hint about her father's prophesy despite the fact that she was exhausted.

One night, while she was working late, she became interested in an especially old file. It mentioned a period of time when the Ukraine was the primary provider of food for the Soviet Union. As she pieced together the missing pieces, a somber and icy conclusion rushed over her. Her father had anticipated not just a territorial takeover, but also a conflict over resources, a fight for nourishment that might spark a war on a global scale. This was not just a geopolitical battle; it was a catastrophe that had the potential to determine the course of humanity's history.

When Anton returned to Belarus, he discovered that he had become a member of a complex network of freedom fighters. Each individual was a vital cog in the resistance's overall mechanism. Their covert defiance was a demonstration of their mother's faith and her hopes for a life of independence. On the other hand, the impending danger of reprisal from the Russian government was a gloomy cloud that hovered over them. The resistance was a ray of light in the darkness, but they were massively outmatched in terms of their numbers and their weapons. They were in need of assistance, and Anton was aware that he needed to make contact with people from all over the world.

Sofia continued to take strength from the memories she shared with her father while she was in Kyiv. Every recollection served as a pedagogical tool for her, a guiding light that helped her through the darkness of war. The tactical know-how she gained while playing chess was now being put to use to protect her city. However, above and beyond the plans and methods, her father's lessons implanted in her an iron will as well as the will to stand against the tyrant and protect her people.

They were each obsessed by the fight, which shaped them, challenged them, and propelled them onward while the echoes of their past resonated in their present. Their histories were not only a source of strength, but also a wellspring of resolve and a catalyst for transformation in their lives. They were now being directed to change the future by the shadows cast by their history.

Each person, despite having their own distinct history, found themselves immersed in a narrative that was far broader than themselves.

A little, unremarkable photograph of a young girl with blonde braids was discovered among the things of Linda's father, and it turned out to be an essential part of the jigsaw. It was Olga, Linda's mother, who came to the United States from Ukraine. She had passed away while Linda was still a little kid, leaving her with only fragmentary memories of her grandmother reading her bedtime tales, singing Ukrainian lullabies, and filling the house with the aroma of freshly made borscht. She now saw why her father was so fascinated by Russia and why he was so driven to learn the country's true objectives. This was really close to my heart. The reverberations of her mother's words turned into a rallying cry for action.

During this time, Anton was using every weapon at his disposal to draw attention to the fact that they were fighting. In his early days as a technology enthusiast, he was a ham radio fanatic. He dusted up an old ham radio set and brought it back to life. Every night, he would send ciphertext messages into the ether, doing his best to keep his fingers crossed that they would be received by the appropriate parties. His eyes, which were set far apart, reflected the sparks from the radio set and twinkled with concentration and determination.

Every night in Kyiv, Sofia would make her rounds across the city while wearing her father's old military coat over her shoulders. The burden of the coat served as a continuous reminder of the importance of her duty. It appeared as though his voice was being carried by the shadows that were being cast by the faint street lights, serving as a guide through the treacherous darkness. During their games of chess, he would advise them to "always be five moves ahead." This knowledge was incorporated into Sofia's strategy at this point, and she was continuously planning, scheming, and attempting to anticipate the actions of the adversary.

They were living in the present because of the past, and the echoes of their history were suggesting the way forward for them. The wounds from their history served as their armor, and the lessons they had learned served as their sword as they fought the wars of today. Even though they were lengthy, the shadows of the past were beginning to shed light on the way to a new dawn.

The CIA headquarters were a busy hive of activity on the other side of the ocean, and Linda's attention was riveted on the satellite footage that was running across her computer. Her gaze followed the wounds that the war had inflicted on the land of her mother's birth, which was a place of old Cossacks, lyrical landscapes, and dogged perseverance. Her recollections of her mother, Olga, shed light on the part she was to play in the struggle at hand, and a wave of determination swept through her. She took another glance at the picture of her mother that was on the wall. It was as though Olga's eyes were saying, "Find the truth, my child." Linda delved back into the mountain of data with a redoubled sense of purpose and resolve.

Anton, ensconced in the claustrophobic confines of his improvised radio room, listened intently to the answer that was laced with static from his previous night's transmission. Every hiss and every crackle might be a crucial piece of information that could save your life. The cramped space was crammed with reminders of his history and served as a temple both to the tech enthusiast he had been in the past and the freedom warrior he had evolved into. The radio set, which had been more of a pastime in the past, had become a symbol of optimism for the people of Belarus and an unseen thread that linked him to the rest of the world.

As Sofia moved stealthily through the night, the streets of Kyiv were foreboding and very cold. The grim reality of battle was a sharp contrast to the military myths that her father had told her. Despite this, she located solace in them. It appeared as though the streets were whispering his methods and his knowledge. She had memorized every street, every corner, and every shady lane because he would always tell her, "Never forget the lay of the land," and she would never forget it. During her alone time, she would hear his voice in her ear like a ghostly guide. This would keep her company.

Their individual histories intertwined with the necessities of the here and now to create the blueprint for their respective foreseeable futures. Their histories were not simply pages in a book that had been closed; rather, they acted as catalysts, providing them with the strength to fight, guiding the decisions they made, and connecting their fates with the destinies of countries. Every action they performed was a reminder of things that had happened in the past, and every choice they made was a gloomy mirror of who they had been in the past. They made their way towards an uncertain but essential future as the past and present danced together in the twilight.

Linda, who was haunted by the last words her mother had spoken to her, combed through the several paperwork that were strewn across her desk. As she rummaged through secret files, secret transcripts, and encrypted messages, the gentle glow of her desk lamp formed long shadows that swirled and flickered as she worked. Each piece of paper, a piece of the jigsaw, got her closer to discovering the truth, which was something that her mother had strongly encouraged her to do. As the night progressed, she found herself thinking back on the life lessons that Olga had ingrained in her, the countless games of chess, and the incessant need to question and investigate. Her mother had been preparing her for this moment without her knowledge, and now her place in the greater scheme of things was starting to become clear.

Anton sat in Belarus, bent over his improvised communication equipment, engrossed in the reverberations of his past. His thoughts meandered back to his youth, when his shelves at home were stacked with books on radio science, and he had a lifelong interest in communication. This preoccupation of his had evolved into a weapon, a lifeline, and a statement of defiance. He tuned in to the frequencies of freedom as his fingers danced around the radio dials. Every static crackle revealed a different story of defiance, bravery, and the unconquerable spirit of the human race. His past, which was full of fantasies of open dialogues, is now entwined with his present and is serving as his light amid the intense gloom.

Sofia made her way through the rubble-strewn lanes and buildings pierced with bullet holes that were littered across the war-torn streets of Kyiv. She was a specter, a watchful sentinel who kept her city secure in silence. Her path was illuminated by the spectral echoes of her father's wartime stories. Each piece of guidance he had offered and each tactic he had divulged acquired a profoundly more significant significance at this point. She was no longer merely a daughter; instead, Sofia had transformed into a soldier, her history and her present coming together to create a fiercely independent fighter.

Their lives had taken a turn that neither of them could have predicted, yet despite this, they held firm, bolstered by the experiences they had shared in the past and by their uncompromising will. They accepted their parts in the larger picture of the struggle as the boundary between the past and the present became increasingly hazy, and they each made a commitment to continue playing their assigned roles right up to the very end. Their histories, their decisions, and their outcomes would all be recorded in the annals of this struggle, leaving long shadows in the sands of time as they passed into history.

Linda broke the silence of her workplace to flip through an old photo album filled with pictures of her family. The light from her desk lamp cast a warm glow that made the dust particles in the air appear to be dancing. She used her fingertips to trace the fading photographs, each one capturing a fleeting moment in time. The young Linda shown in the images smiled, unaware of the complex web of mystery that was about to encircle her life. Now, she longed for the innocence she had back then, but the sharp corners of reality and the burden of her obligation had taken it away from her. Her concentration was riveted on a photograph of Olga, her mother. She put on her regular hard attitude, but there was a spark of knowledge that Linda had always liked in her eyes, despite the fact that she was wearing her typical harsh expression. She had been more to her than just a mother; she had also been her teacher and her director. Following her mother's passing, Linda found herself in unfamiliar land, with only the memories and life lessons that her mother had taught her to use as a compass.

During this time, Anton was hiding out in the basement of a house that had been abandoned, listening to the faint buzz of his makeshift radio equipment. Even though he was worn out physically, his mind was still active, and memories were moving quickly through it. He reflected on his father, a severe individual who valued order, self-control, and the quest for knowledge. Anton's interest in communication was nurtured by the presence of books and radio equipment in his room, which served as a haven for Anton. A specific recollection came back to him at that moment: his very first radio transmission that was successful. When his father glanced at him, he noticed a fleeting twinge of pride in his eyes. He was twelve years old. His father had taught him how to do it when he was young, and it had been more of a pastime for him back then, but now it was an essential ability for staying alive. He was using it to help the resistance.

Under the cover of night, Sofia moved stealthily through the bombed-out streets of Kyiv, which is located on the other side of the border. She could practically hear the echoes of her father's words; vivid pictures being painted in her mind by the tales he told of his time in the military. He was an officer who had received several decorations for his bravery and strategic genius. His tales were more than just entertaining yarns; they were teachings that helped shape Sofia into the warrior she was destined to become. She recalled how his eyes would light up whenever he talked of bravery, honor, or duty. These words served as her compass now, the spirit of her father alive and well within her as she faced the dangers of the battlefield.

Their histories were reflected in the acts they were taking at the current time, which was a monument to their resiliency and the legacy that their ancestry had left behind. They had become unsung heroes without realizing it in a war that went beyond the scope of their individual lives, and now each of them carried the weight of their history while directing the path of their future.

The tale of their lives was woven into the fabric of their lives like a tapestry, and each thread and knot had a different story and a different lesson.

Linda analyzed an old photograph of her mother's face by following the contours of her mother's face as they appeared in the picture. Olga, with her flaming red hair and ice blue eyes, had been the epitome of paradoxes; she was a force of nature that had a great impact on her daughter. Her daughter's life has been profoundly influenced by her mother. Linda's attention was drawn to a photograph showing the two of them participating in a demonstration. The inscription on the placard that Olga was holding said "NO NUKES, KNOW PEACE." Even though she was only seven years old at the time, she recalled the passion in her mother's voice and the resolve in her mother's eyes even though it was her first exposure to the world of politics. These principles had acted as a compass for Linda's journey, directing her toward a career in the CIA and shaping her into the analyst that she was today.

In order to keep himself warm, Anton clung to his memories of the past in his chilly cellar. His thoughts meandered back to a wintry evening when he was a boy, specifically the day when his father gave him a radio receiver that he had manufactured himself. Even though it was just a simple gadget, the small boy thought of it as a priceless treasure. His father had taken the time to teach him the nuances of radio transmission, which served as the spark that ultimately pushed him to pursue a career as a freedom fighter. The radio, which had been constructed by his father, was now his sword and shield; it had become a weapon of resistance.

The events of Sofia's past were carved into her mind and her recollections were burned into her very being. A dramatic contrast to the tranquil and idyllic environment in which she had grown up was provided by the war-torn streets of Kyiv. However, the bravery that she had gained from her father served as a source of inspiration for her. She recalled her father taking her under his wing and teaching her how to shoot, his authoritative voice directing her. "Aim with your mind, pull the trigger with your heart," he'd told them. These instructions had turned her into a powerful soldier, and she had continued her father's legacy by carrying out his orders.

Their histories had molded their present, and their ancestors had directed the course of their destinies. Every movement that they made was a memorial to their forebears and a declaration of the heritage that was carried in their veins. Each win and defeat were a piece of their history that was resurrected and brought into the present, like a specter of their past leaving its imprint on the here and now.

Linda's eyes began to flood up with tears as she continued to look at the picture of her mother. Olga's life was cut short by a sudden illness despite the fact that she had a fiery personality. After her mother passed away, Linda was left with the duty of carrying on her mother's legacy of searching for peace in a world that is frequently marred by strife. Even though her supervisors disregarded her suspicions about the violence in Eastern Europe, she was encouraged to investigate the matter more by the sound of her mother's words, which continued to ring in her ears.

Anton opened a little, old box when he was down in the damp cellar. On the inside was an old photograph of him and his father, in which they are both beaming broadly and the family radio can be seen in the center of their grins. Anton recalled the gleam that used to shine in his father's eyes, as well as the hearty laughter that used to reverberate throughout the little workshop that they had established in their basement. Anton's destiny was unintentionally put in motion by his father, who worked as a radio engineer. As a result, Anton was equipped with information that would later help him save lives. Anton pressed the photograph to his chest and drew courage from the recollections of a period when serenity was not a luxury item but rather a given.

On the other hand, Sofia was sitting on the edge of her crib, holding on to an ancient medal that had lost most of its shine. It was a medal that her father had been awarded for his service in a war that took place a long time before she was born. As she recalled the tales her father had told her when she was younger about bravery and making sacrifices, the metal in her grip began to feel warmer. These stories did not conclude with rousing victories or heroes who emerged victorious. They were able to make it through the ordeal, save the lives of those they cared about, and keep their composure in the face of hardship. This medal served as her talisman at this point, as well as her link to her father, whose lessons she exemplified while serving on the battlefield.

Their histories did not drag them down; rather, they were a source of power for them. These recollections, these experiences, were invaluable pieces of their identities; they were linked with their very selves and served as a compass for them as they navigated the treacherous terrain of life. Every choice they made and action they did was not just their own, but also the realization of the aspirations and ambitions of those who had come before them.

As the evening advanced, darker shadows began to cover everything in the globe. As the din of the war receded into the distance, the three found that they were lured back into their respective pasts in an effort to find solace and fortitude there.

When Linda was in Washington, she could get a glimpse of her mother's spirit in the flame of the candle that was lit next to her bed. She recalled her mother's words: "The world is not as black and white as you make it out to be, Linda. It's a kaleidoscope of different shades of gray." The intricacies of the universe were clearer to Linda as a result of the wisdom that she possessed. It provided her the tenacity to dive deeper into the murky politics of the fight and the bravery to question the complacency of her superiors. Additionally, it armed her with the tenacity to go deeper into the dark politics of the battle. She was more than just an analyst for the CIA. She was the daughter of her mother, and she fought for a world that was liberated from the shackles of war.

Anton discovered comfort in the warm tones of the outdated

family portrait, which was located thousands of miles distant from him. He could almost hear the crackle of the radio and his father's delighted voice as they tuned in to broadcasts from all across the world as he brushed his fingertips over the fading image. In a world that was becoming more violent all the time, he found solace in the fact that he could spend his boyhood working with radio equipment. Due to the fact that he possessed such expertise, he was an essential asset to the Ukrainian resistance. He was not just a freedom warrior in Belarus; he was also his father's son, and he used his father's wisdom to impede the progress of the adversary.

In the ruined city of Kyiv, Sofia clung to the medal that her father had won as if it were a lifeline. She could almost feel her father's enormous, calloused hands embracing her little ones as she traced the worn-out inscription, and she could hear her father's soothing voice speaking stories of bravery and self-sacrifice. She was no longer interested in hearing such ridiculous tales. They were a part of the everyday experience that she had, a heritage that she continued to uphold. She was not just a soldier, but she was also a daughter who took pride in being resolute in the face of hardship much like her father.

As their histories were pieced together, revealing the roads they had traveled and the roads they had yet to go, the specters of conflict began to materialize. However, these shadows were no match for the unyielding spirits of our characters, who were each motivated by a history that would not be forgotten and a future that held the hope of atonement.

As the night fell, enveloping the globe in a cloak of darkness, each of our heroes was rooted in their recollections, the experiences they had in the past lighting the torches that would enlighten their routes as they traveled through the darkness. They were all a living testimony to their ancestry and the upbringing that had been passed down to them from generation to generation. The reverberations of their histories combined with the deafening roars of battle to produce a symphony that was equally eerie and motivating.

Their histories were connected because they were molded by the unrelenting beat of a single adversary, despite the fact that they were separated by miles of territory and great political chasms. A force that was icy and calculated, and its goal was to bury their unique identities beneath a tide of ruin. However, these powers had grossly miscalculated the strength of the human spirit, namely the tenacity that is developed out of love, grief, and sacrifice.

The seeds of resistance took root in the heart of Washington, D.C., the whispering streets of Minsk, and the beleaguered alleyways of Kyiv, all of which were nurtured by the echoes of their own histories. The events of the day had left an indelible stamp on their spirits, the memories of their own successes and losses now carved into the very fabric of their lives by which they lived. And as the moon made its way across the dark sky in a silvery arc, our heroes, each in their own unique manner, prepared themselves for the difficulties that were still to come. They were each prepared to face the brightness of the dawn and the uncertainty that would come with another day spent in the battlefield, having been fueled by the darkness of their own histories.

Even though the veil of night had descended, the spirit of resistance was in no way concealed. The reverberations of the past remained, sculpting the outlines of a future that was unknown yet hopeful.

CHAPTER 8 "A NEW FRONT"

After the harsh siege that had been placed on Kyiv, the Ukrainian troops had gathered up a feeling of urgency and commitment to liberate the city. The shrieks of the dead and the screams of the injured had coalesced into a chorus of resiliency, which inspired the men and women of the land to stand and fight. It was an emotional infection, a surge of optimism and determination that coursed through the veins of the formerly downtrodden troops, and it spread across the entire group.

As a result, the Ukrainian troops, which were commanded by the seasoned General Petrovich and assisted by the orange glow of dawn, marched towards the northeast in order to establish a new front. There were soldiers in green uniforms scattered throughout the fields in Eastern Ukraine. Their faces were set in grim resolve, and their pulses were pounding with a mix of terror and eagerness.

At the same time, on the other side of the ocean, CIA analyst Emily Hastings was sitting in her office with the lights turned down low, perusing the most recent batch of intelligence files. As she looked at the satellite photos, there was a palpable sense of tension in the room. The only sound in the otherwise silent space was the low hum of the computer fan.

She came to an abrupt halt as her gaze landed on a picture of an apparently unremarkable freight train winding its way across the frozen expanses of Siberia. But something didn't seem quite right about it. Her interest was sparked when she noticed a string of unmarked military-grade vehicles being put onto the freight train.

Emily came upon a disturbing piece of information while she was doing a cross-reference of the photos with data from a broad variety of sources. It was a new generation of hypersonic missile technology that was being placed onto the trucks. This technology was meant to disrupt and defeat the most advanced of defense systems.

If the data was correct, the Russians had the intention of employing this new weapon to swing the battle in their favor and turn the tide of the conflict in their favor. This was no longer your run-of-the-mill warfare. The stakes were raised, and the level of risk was significantly increased.

Emily had the impression that the entire world was resting on her shoulders. Because of the intelligence she possessed, not only might the battle be fought differently, but also perhaps thousands of lives may be spared. She hurriedly grabbed her notes, and then ran out of her office, heading in the direction of the director's office. Her pulse was thumping in her chest, each beat resonating with the significance of the realization.

A new day had broken, not only with a fresh front on the combat, but also in the mysterious realm of international espionage. The situation was becoming more and more complicated. The shadows of the past continued to hover over the present, but the determination of these individuals began to chisel a way ahead, creating a shard of hope that punctured the veils that were covering a deadly battle.

Emily's heels made a clicking sound on the marble floor as she went down the long corridor of the CIA headquarters. Her mind was working like a well-oiled machine. Not just for the forces of Ukraine, but also for the global power dynamics that were then in play, the consequences of the finding that she had discovered were enormous. If Russia had the capability to launch hypersonic missiles, the stakes would have been significantly different.

When we last left General Petrovich, he was in the midst of a strategic discussion with his lieutenants in Ukraine. The huge map that covered the whole table was dotted with numerous markers, some of which represented their troops while others indicated the locations of the adversary. The grim determination that could be seen on everyone's face around the table was evidence that even though their strategy was ambitious and carried more than its fair share of dangers, they were prepared to carry it through nonetheless.

Petrovich had much of experience in the battlefield. Both his father and he had served in several peacekeeping operations all over the world, with the former serving in Afghanistan. He also had served in a number of these missions. He wore his war wounds, both apparent and unseen, as badges of pride, as a reminder of the conflicts he had fought and the allies he had lost. However, this conflict was not like the others; it was a battle to save their territory and preserve their way of life.

Petrovich couldn't help but feel a sense of satisfaction as he moved the marker he was using on the map to the northern front of the northeastern sector. He was leading his soldiers into a fight that would go down in the annals of their history as a monument to their bravery and resiliency in the face of adversity.

Emily, who was located thousands of miles away, ran into the office of the director with her heart pounding and her cheeks reddened as a result of the importance of the discovery she had just made. She did a rapid explanation of her results as she spread the satellite photographs out on the director's desk. The expression on the director's face tightened as he listened, and the director's eyes became sterner as he came to the conclusion. Emily was given a stern nod, and he promised to take prompt action based on the facts she had provided.

Emily was unable to release the tightness that had become knotted up in her gut as the door closed behind her. She had done what was expected of her, but the rest was out of her control at this point. She was experiencing agitation, and as she made her way back to her office, she glanced at the clock that was hanging on the wall. It looked like we were in for a very long night.

Petrovich and his soldiers rallied their spirits with a fresh sense of purpose, and they returned to the front lines of the Ukrainian conflict ready to continue their advance into the northeast. The biting bite of the icy winter wind on their faces did little to dampen their resoluteness in the face of the challenge. They were aware that the path that lay in front of them was laden with perils, but they were also aware that they were the final line of defense for their country.

The wheels of battle continued to churn, but in the middle of the mayhem and uncertainty, threads of hope and resolution were being sewn, portraying a picture of tenacity and constancy in the face of adversity. The remnants of the past continued to collide with the facts of the present, which had the effect of reshaping the trajectory of the future.

Under the cover of darkness, Ukrainian soldiers started their advance on the enemy territory. The pitch blackness was occasionally broken up by flashes of flares and tracers, but the soldiers did not waver in their determination as they moved forward like a wave of unstoppable willpower.

While everything was going on, Emily kept working through her analysis with her fingers moving quickly over the keyboard. Her displays flashed with encoded data and satellite pictures, depicting a complicated tapestry of army movements and geopolitical maneuvers. Her screens were connected to a network. She tracked the patterns of the adversary's design with each stroke of the keypad, feeling the pressure of her revelation grow with each passing moment.

When they got back to the war room, Petrovich immediately turned his attention to the map of the northeastern front. They were engaging in a risky maneuver by creating a new front, which had the potential to spread out the Russian forces and make them more vulnerable. However, the stakes were enormous; all it would take was a single error in judgment for them to fall into the hands of their adversary.

As the hours passed on, there was a noticeable increase in the level of tension on both fronts. The staging area for the Ukrainian forces' advance to the northeastern front had been successfully achieved. The night was filled with murmurings and the sound of clothing being rustled. They waited for the morning to break so that they would know it was safe to advance and regain their territory.

Emily was in a time crunch as she made her way across the Atlantic Ocean. Her research had uncovered a network of subterranean bunkers that were believed to house the purported hypersonic weapons. The repercussions were really serious. She was aware that she needed to bring this information to light as soon as possible since the power dynamic was altering.

Petrovich's troops made their move as soon as the sun began to rise. The previously peaceful morning descended into a whirlwind of gunshots and smoke in an instant. The sound of tanks charging into enemy territory filled the air, and the sunshine caught the metallic sheen of the vehicles as they moved forward.

As the conflict continued, Petrovich's communications equipment alerted him to the receipt of a coded message. He focused his eyes intently on the display, trying to comprehend the encrypted message. As he received the letter from Emily, which revealed the existence of the hypersonic missiles, his pupils drew together and his eyes expanded.

Petrovich felt a thumping sensation in his chest caused by his heart. The stakes had, in point of fact, shifted. The news, although disheartening, also offered a ray of optimism in the situation. If they were successful in taking control of these bunkers, it would give them a significant advantage in the conflict.

The drums of battle continued to beat, and those involved in the struggle kept dancing. Their entwined destinies were being written with each passing instant, and it didn't matter where they were: on the freezing frontlines of Ukraine or in the busy offices of the CIA.

In the middle of the intense fighting, Ukrainian forces pushed forward in a determined manner. As they made their way through the labyrinth of trenches and defenses, the ground trembled beneath their feet, and their hearts pounded in time with the rhythm of their advance. Each explosion and each bullet served as a staccato note in the symphony that was their rebellion.

While all was going on, Emily was competing against the clock. The disclosure of the missile bunkers had set her into a frenzy, and she had been working nonstop ever since. Her eyes darted between the many screens as she juggled the jobs with a frenzied intensity, and she frantically tried to communicate the coordinates to Petrovich's squad.

Petrovich stood over the war table at the most crucial part of the Ukrainian command post, with his eyes following the course of the conflict as it developed. The information that Emily sent along was extremely important. Petrovich swiftly sent the locations to his field commanders while giving commands with a resolute and unyielding spirit. The strategy was being adjusted on the fly; an audacious assault on the missile bunkers had become the primary objective.

The soldiers were given their instructions when they were out in the field. They could not believe what they were seeing, but there was no time for them to be afraid. The tanks started up with a roar, churning the snow-covered ground beneath their massive treads as they steered themselves in the direction of the new targets. The infantry did the same thing, and their breath misted up in the chilly air as they prepared for the next push.

Emily was sitting at her desk at the CIA holding her breath as she watched the satellite broadcast. The little blips on the screen, which represented Ukrainian soldiers, started moving towards the bunkers. As she observed their development, the passage of time appeared to slow down, and each second felt like an eternity. She had done everything that was in her power, and the rest was now in their hands.

The battlefield was awash with strong contrasts of light and shadow, as well as life and death, as the first light of dawn gave way to the harsh light of day. The Ukrainian soldiers proceeded steadily in the direction of their objective, their resolve remaining unshaken in spite of the terrible resistance they faced.

The conflict became more intense as the day progressed. Tanks fought against emplacements that had been strengthened, soldiers maneuvered through a lethal tapestry of gunfire and artillery, and the constant hum of planes flying overhead presented a bleak image of the breadth of the battle.

Nevertheless, despite the fire and fury, the men and women fighting on both fronts continued to advance. They negotiated the chaotic landscape of battle, bound by duty and propelled by hope, their hearts echoing the pounding of their collective will: to fight, to survive, and to win.

The next morning brought with it a brisk wind that tore through the layers of clothing as well as the flesh of those who were outside. The battlefield was littered with the remnants of yesterday's fighting, but the Ukrainian forces had little time to reflect because they were under constant threat of attack. They moved behind the protection of their armored vehicles, keeping their grim expressions and their hearts aflame as they prepared for another round of combat.

The silhouette of the missile bunkers could be seen on the horizon as the sun began to rise. They looked like enormous tombs that portended impending disaster. However, the Ukrainian troops did not let this dissuade them from their goal, and they continued to press forward. They pushed forward with a tenacity that could only come from the combination of desperation and bravery, pushing as their tanks and smoke grenades provided cover for them from the oncoming enemy fire.

Emily had her eyes riveted to her screen when she got back to Washington. Every blip and every dot stood for a life, a heartbeat, and a glimmer of hope. The anxiety was real; it wrapped itself around her like a suffocating garment, causing each breath to be shorter and each instant to be longer. She was well aware that every moment was very important and that the information she supplied may tip the balance either way.

Yelena got a message from Emily that was encoded when she was in Minsk. She was wary, but she knew she had to put her faith in her contact. She then shared the information with her network of people involved in the resistance, praying all the while that it would be enough. She stood there, watching as communications shot back and forth between two different parties, her heart beating in time with the ticking of the clock. Every ally counted now since the conflict was being fought on several fronts in addition to the battlefield itself.

While all was going on, Petrovich was right in the middle of the chaos, ordering his soldiers with an iron determination. His words served as a beacon that cut through the haze of battle, and his voice served as the rock upon which his troops anchored their will. The tanks reorganized themselves under his direction, taking the shape of a spearhead that sliced through the opposing forces' lines and inched closer to the bunkers with each passing second.

The landscape was difficult, and the adversary was unrelenting. However, the Ukrainians fought like madmen throughout the whole conflict. They moved forward at a rapid pace, leaving in their path the charred and burning remnants of enemy vehicles. This served as a marker for their progress.

On the battlefield, Ivan was commanding a squad of his troops as they moved from one crater to another, keeping their bodies pressed closely against the uneven ground. They had sweat and filth mingled on their cheeks, hard breathing, and their hands were solid on the guns they were holding. They were quite clear about their aim, which was to take down the missile bunkers. A risky move that may alter the overall direction of the conflict.

As the conflict continued, the Ukrainian troops continued to make progress toward the goal they had set for themselves. The missile bunkers appeared to be unassailable fortresses, yet it was necessary for them to be captured. The futures of entire countries were up in the air. They bore the load of that obligation, which was rather heavy, but they carried it all the same - not as a hardship, but as a badge of pride.

As a result, the Ukrainian soldiers engaged in combat despite the loud boom of the artillery and the rattling sound of the gunfire. The battlefield was bathed in a harsh, spectral light as a result of each explosion, and the lengthy shadows formed by the explosions moved and flickered in response to each flash. Every single soldier stood out like a silhouette against the chaos, and they were all heroes in their own right. They did not fight for glory, nor did they fight for notoriety; rather, they battled for the place that they called home. because the future was still something that was worth fighting for.

Emily observed the simulated landscape of the conflict by looking at it through the lens of her computer screen. The map was made up of blips and blobs that indicated people, vehicles, encampments, and sites respectively. Taking into account the human toll that is being exacted in the here and now, there was a coldness to it that suggested callousness. Her gaze was intently directed on the north-eastern front. This was the point at which the new front lines were established. The area that will be the focus of the subsequent massive attack.

Emily's employment has undergone several changes. It was no longer sufficient to merely collect and analyze the intelligence anymore. She had the impression that she had become an essential component of the Ukrainian resistance, giving them the understanding, they had to make a comeback and recapture their territory. She painstakingly examined each pixel on her screen while simultaneously running simulations and algorithms in an effort to locate any potential advantage that the Ukrainian military may take advantage of.

Her attention was drawn to a pattern in the enemy's movement. She moved closer to the conversation while her mind raced furiously. If her assumption was correct, then she could have found a weakness in the defenses put up by the Russians. An essential piece of knowledge that, if it were to be revealed, would likely swing the battle in favor of the Ukrainian troops.

In Kiev, Yelena was assisting in the organization of the resistance movement and getting the fighters ready for the impending attack. Their weapons were rudimentary, and they had received only rudimentary instruction, yet their spirits remained unshaken. The knowledge that Emily had provided had provided them with something that they had been lacking for some time now: hope. It had become their most powerful weapon at this point.

The Ukrainian troops had been able to make substantial advancements on the front that was located in the northeast. They fought using a strategy that combined guerrilla warfare with more conventional methods while under Petrovich's command. The bunkers could now be seen in the distance. As the tanks rumbled closer, the troops' hearts began to beat in time with each other, a rhythmic demonstration of their unyielding determination.

However, the Russian forces were in no way close to becoming victorious. The Ukrainians were forced to seek shelter as they were subjected to a hailstorm of gunfire and rockets that were launched from the bunkers. After then, there was a vicious confrontation since neither side was ready to back down. The tension was thick in the air, and there was also a strong odor of expended gunfire.

Ivan maintained his composure during the entirety of this confrontation. His eyes glowed with a ferocious determination that not even the bloodiest conflict could put out. As he moved through the landscape that had been ravaged by conflict, he dragged the responsibility of his nation's future behind him. Despite this, he maintained his erect posture. He was well aware that the fate of millions of people depended on their accomplishment, and he understood that failure was not an option.

Emily's fingers were flying over the keyboard as she relayed the information to her contacts in Ukraine while she was back in Washington. Her whole body was tense with concentration as her eyes were fixed on the television in front of her. Even though she was hundreds of miles distant from the battleground, she was nearly able to hear the crackling of gunfire, the thundering booms of the tanks, and the roaring engines of the armored motor trucks.

It's possible that she was physically secure in her office, but emotionally, she was in the thick of the war. She had a twinge of melancholy each time a blip vanished from the display on her screen. Despite this, she was aware that the intelligence she was supplying was making a difference and assisting Ukrainian forces in driving the invaders back and reclaiming their territory.

This was no longer merely a fight for Ukraine; rather, it was a fight for freedom and justice. And for as long as she was able to be of assistance, Emily would. There was too much riding on the outcome to take any other action.

Ivan's commands reverberated over the chaos of the battlefield, reverberating off the broken ruins of what was once a vibrant hamlet on the northeastern front. As he spoke, his army surged forward like a well-oiled machine, navigating the onslaught of hostile fire with a seamless combination of premeditated maneuvers and instinctive responses. Their military training, their willpower, and their natural instincts all come together to form a lethal dance of combat.

As he saw his warriors perish, it broke his heart, yet despite their setbacks, their determination only appeared to grow stronger. They were battling for the survival of themselves, their families, and the country that they called home. And each loss of life appeared to fortify their resolve, with the result being an increased sense of determination on the battlefield.

A message was received among all of the mayhem that was going on. Emily. Her voice, unmistakable and unwavering, cut through the cacophony of the battleground, bringing with it the expectation and determination of a whole people. There was more than simply intelligence contained in the material that she shared. In the midst of overwhelming hopelessness, it served as a savior and a ray of light.

In his head, a plan began to take shape, one that would allow them to turn Emily's information to their advantage. He gave a terse command, and immediately the gears began to turn. Emily had found a weak spot in the Russian lines, and a handful of troops, quick and nimble, began to creep their way in that direction in order to avoid detection.

When Yelena got back to the bunker, she listened intently to the updates that came over the communications system while holding her breath. Her heart was thumping in her chest, and the rhythm of the battle outside could be heard in each and every pulse. The calm that prevailed within the bunker stood in sharp contrast to the commotion that could be heard just a few miles away during the fierce struggle.

While she was listening to Ivan's commands, her imagination

conjured up a clear image of the battlefield, complete with Ivan's stern expression and the unyielding resolve of their warriors. The anxiety was almost unbearable, and the stakes were quite high. In spite of all that was going on, there was still a sliver of optimism. The knowledge that Emily provided, which was an essential part of her commitment to their war effort, was making a difference.

Emily, who was in Washington, watched as the computerized image of the battleground changed. She could see Ivan's plan coming to fruition, with the troops making their way towards the vulnerable spot that she had spotted. It was a last-ditch effort, a high-stakes gamble that had the potential to alter the course of the whole conflict.

Emily felt an influx of optimism as she saw the blips travel across her screen as she watched the video. She was involved in this process. Her efforts were making a positive impact. Her dedication to this important work was made clear with each new piece of information that she shared and with every life that she may have helped to save.

Emily could only pray that the information she provided and the contributions she made would be sufficient as she watched the conflict unfold before her. A sufficient amount to reverse the trend and provide Ukraine with the advantage it required. Because as she was seeing the combat taking place in cyberspace, she came to the conclusion that this conflict was about more than simply Ukraine. It was a battle for democracy's fundamental survival, as well as for individual liberty and judicial fairness.

Ivan kept a close eye on how his gamble turned out when he was on the front lines. As Emily had predicted, his troops advanced until they reached the vulnerable spot, which turned out to be an artillery station with inadequate defenses. The little crew concealed themselves in the darkness and inched their way closer to the poorly guarded enemy position. It was a dance of life and death set to the gruesome melody of war, and each step that was performed required a careful balance between quiet and speed.

As Ivan watched his troops advance, his eyes were transfixed to the binoculars he was holding, and the stress in his hands caused his knuckles to become white. The commander of the group signaled to his soldiers with a nod that they needed to be ready for the assault. Ivan's heart was beating, and he tightened his grasp on the binoculars. The following few minutes would be extremely important, serving as the deciding factor in a key strategy that relied totally on Emily's wits.

Emily's eyes were glued to the screen the entire time she was back in Washington, where the infrared pictures were playing a pixelated version of the deadly gamble. The dots in green, which represented Ivan's crew, proceeded like ghosts through the darkness in the direction of the symbol in red, which represented the Russian artillery station. The deep calm that pervaded the room was broken only by the faint clicks made by her coworkers as they worked at their stations and the quiet hum of the large computers. The tension was apparent, and it felt as though someone were praying in silence. In the event that Ivan's group was successful, they would hold a major advantage on this newly opened front. If they were unsuccessful...

Emily made a motion with her head to indicate that she did not want to consider that idea. She had finished what was expected of her; she had provided them with everything she could. Ivan and his soldiers were the only ones who could win now.

While Yelena listened to the reports on the progress that were being broadcast over the radio in the bunker, she held her breath. The static-filled stillness that would ensue between reports was almost as excruciating as the sounds of the conflict that was now being fought. Her heart would race every time she heard the familiar crackle of the radio coming to life.

Suddenly, there was a flurry of recent information arriving all at once. "We've moved into position... We're actively engaging... Objective accomplished!"

There was rejoicing all across the command center, with yells of happiness and relief reverberating off the walls of the bunker. The plan had been successful. Ivan's group had accomplished their mission of seizing the enemy artillery installation, which resulted in a decisive victory on the new front.

However, their triumph did not come without a price. There were still some people who had not returned. A sobering reminder that the shadows of war spared no one, not even in the midst of victory. Each setback, a personal tragedy, strengthened their will to persevere. This was their war, and this was their home, and they were going to defend it with their lives till the very end.

Ivan stood still amidst the commotion of the festivities that followed the victorious attack on the enemy stronghold. As he took in the information of the casualties, his face became pale, and a scowl was permanently imprinted onto his features. Four people were killed, and two others were injured. Each name, each defeat was a blow that chipped away at his determination and tested the tenacity of his character.

Emily, now back in the United States, was not oblivious to the price that had been paid for their win. The cryptic green and red dots that appeared on her screen represented real individuals whose lives had been irreversibly altered or cut short as a result of the sacrifices made in the sake of their nation. She was well aware of the toll that the war had taken. She was reminded of the words that her mentor had spoken to her as the thrill of her triumph began to wear off: "Every piece of intel, every call we make, lives hang in the balance."

While all was going on, Yelena was working in the Ukrainian command center, and she could hear the cheers coming from the room. But despite all of the joy she was experiencing, she had a chilling fear. They were victorious, but the capture of the German artillery station did not come without a price. She made a solemn oath to herself as she tightened her hands to ensure that the lives that were taken would not be in vain.

Their individual tragedies were a heavy burden for each of them, which served to strengthen their commitment and fire their determination. It was no longer merely a game of chess strategy; instead, it had taken on a more personal tone. They would never be the same after the war, and there was no turning back.

When morning finally rose over the besieged city of Kyiv, the new front was already ablaze with the sparks of defiance from the rebels. A symbol of fortitude and perseverance in the face of tragedy, the flag of Ukraine fluttered proudly over the artillery station that had been taken. Every success, every failure, and every sacrifice were a stepping stone that brought them that much closer to achieving their objective.

The last of the rebels stirred in the darkness as they plotted their next move. They moved like phantoms, attacking the adversary with fresh fervor, and were guided in their efforts by Anatoly, who had supplied them with priceless data. Their acts of defiance and resiliency reverberated throughout the front and served as a rallying cry for the Ukrainian army.

As the day progressed, the new front transformed into a symbol of the resistance of the Ukrainian people. With each passing hour, it served as a demonstration of their unwavering spirit and their unwavering will to see the situation through. They could all sense that the tide was about to turn. Their individual triumphs and defeats were woven into the greater fabric of the war, which ultimately determined the path that the fight would take.

Despite this, the conflict was not even close to being ended at this point. There were still wars to be fought, sacrifices to be made, and tales to be told. All of these things were still to come. This was only the beginning of a new front, a new chapter in their fight for freedom, and they were only getting started.

The gears of war were spinning, and each individual was a cog in the machine; the tales of these characters were interweaving in a dance that was as complex as it was perilous. Anatoly, who was now a full-fledged member of the Ukrainian resistance, found himself back in the city that he had previously called home. His familiarity with the local topography proved to be a great asset to the guerrilla warfare that they were engaged in. Emily, via the eyes of her drones and the data from her reports, sensed that the normally antiseptic ambience of the CIA headquarters was permeated with a feeling of urgency and danger. Yelena and Ivan, who were in charge of the frontline, felt the constant strain that comes with being in a position of leadership since the decisions they made would have a direct impact on the lives of the people they were responsible for.

Anatoly learned of the victory of the Ukrainian army through the conversation that was broadcast over the radio. He was well aware of what this meant, which was that their adversary would be on high alert, making the position he held in the resistance an even more dangerous one. However, this was his town and his house. His intimate knowledge of the slender passageways, secret shortcuts, and shadowy places to hide proved to be quite useful. Every structure sheltered a recollection, and every nook and cranny of the neighborhood housed a fragment of his history. And at this point, every place was of critical importance to their effort to win their freedom.

At the same time, back at the CIA headquarters, Emily was examining a fresh batch of data that had only recently been received. Satellite imaging, radio communications, and the movements of the troops were some of the pieces of the puzzle that were beginning to fit together. Her attention was drawn to a peculiarity in the report, which consisted of a number of scrambled radio transmissions coming from a place that ought to have been abandoned. It was unobtrusive, making it simple to overlook among the mayhem of the war. But Emily had an excellent eye for the little things. As she began to comprehend what this may imply, she felt a palpitation in her chest. It's possible that this will be the break they've been waiting for, the turning point in their fight.

Ivan and Yelena were both dealing with their own set of problems while stationed on the Ukrainian battlefield. The elation they felt after their first win had worn off, and they were now faced with the sobering truth of their predicament. Even though they had triumphed in one engagement, the conflict was far from ended. Their warriors had been fighting for a long time without rest, and their resources were running low. In spite of the unfavorable conditions, there was a fierce resolve in each of their eyes that would not be shaken.

Ivan inhaled deeply as he focused his attention on the map that was laid out in front of him. Each marker denoted a different unit, or a group of men and women working together under his direction. He felt the weight of the duty on his shoulders, but he also knew that he could not afford to give in to the pressure. He turned his attention to Yelena, whose features were illuminated by the weak light. She was bringing comfort to the soldiers and boosting their spirit with the words that she was speaking. Her unyielding will and resolute fortitude were qualities that he couldn't help but respect. They were in this together, and they were going to stick it out until the very end.

Emily realized that she was onto something after she got back to Washington, D.C. She stayed up all night poring through the information, with just the gentle hum of her laptop providing any kind of company in her isolated office. She had been investigating a series of peculiar data packets, and they were all pointing in the same direction: an unexpected and considerable buildup of military forces. She may have been hundreds of miles away from the front lines, but she could still feel the tension in the air. She was aware that she needed to move quickly. A hastily arranged conference with her supervisors was called for, during which she reported her results while stressing the importance of the number of lives that might be saved or lost based on each fact and figure.

In the meantime, Anatoly was on his own quest through the destroyed streets of Kyiv. He engaged in a perilous game of cat and mouse with the opposing troops, using his in-depth familiarity with the city as a compass and his unyielding attitude as his guide. His mission was to report on the movements of the troops as well as any potential choke spots that the Ukrainian forces may take advantage of. There was a certain sarcastic poetry to his deed; once at a time, he had walked these streets as a boy, naïve to the war games performed by world powers, and now, he was a pawn in the same games, fighting for his hometown. His actions had a certain poetic quality to them.

As Ivan and Yelena led their men deeper into enemy territory in the north-eastern region of the map, the severity of the fight increased. The terrain was foreign, and the adversary's resistance was far more than anticipated. Their determination remained unshaken in spite of the setbacks. They were aware that they were heading in the correct direction. The wins were not won easily, but with each one they moved closer to their ultimate objective, which was the liberation of their motherland.

Yelena and her other field commanders were gathered together under the shelter of the night, with their faces just barely discernible in the dim light cast by the tactical map. Their eyes revealed tales of wars waged, friends lost, and victories achieved. Their eyes conveyed stories. Her soul hurt for them, but she realized they could not afford to mourn the losses they had suffered at this time. Not yet. Their plan was fraught with peril, but it was also their greatest chance for success. It was imperative that we act quickly.

As the hours progressed into days, each of our characters went through the emotional ups and downs of battle, including the wins that gave them a surge of adrenaline, the defeats that crushed their spirits, and the lulls in the action that allowed them to reflect on the gravity of their predicament. Every choice they made and every move they made moved them one step closer to altering the path that this battle would take. However, at what expense? The only way to find out is to wait.

Emily's disclosure regarding the Russian military buildup has sparked a series of occurrences right in the middle of Washington, District of Columbia. Conversations spoken in hushed tones in dimly lit nooks of the Pentagon, briefings with the President that took place behind closed doors, and the swift mobilization of the intelligence community all occurred simultaneously. Her finding was not merely a significant step forward; rather, it was a ticking time bomb that had the potential to change the course of the fight.

Emily's discovery of vital information was sent to the Ukrainian intelligence service in the form of a coded message that was sent across a CIA-controlled secure channel. The communication was encrypted. A cop opened the letter when he was located thousands of miles away in a room that was filled with smoke. As he read the words, the tension in his face increased. His hand went to the radio, and he made a call to set up an urgent gathering. Tension and unanswered questions filled the air like a buzzing beehive.

Ivan and Yelena, who were stationed on the northern front, were beginning to feel the pressure. The uncharted landscape was perilous and full of things that couldn't be predicted. However, there were others around them. They took on each obstacle with the support of their comrades, forging an unbreakable relationship thanks to the common resiliency they all had. Every setback served as a test, and every improvement constituted a win. Even though it was battered and bloodstained from the conflict, the Ukrainian flag continued to fly high, serving as a symbol of their unbreakable will.

Anatoly carried on with his dangerous assignment right in the middle of Kyiv. Each shady backstreet and concealed nook presented a fresh conundrum that needed to be solved. The adversary was there in all places but nowhere in particular. In order to avoid being seen by enemy patrols, he slipped stealthily through the shadows while gathering information to relay to the Ukrainian soldiers. Anatoly was not only able to help his people with each successful mission, but he was also able to uncover a side of himself that he was unaware even existed - a courageous warrior who was willing to do whatever it needed to preserve his hometown.

The tension was reaching a boiling point. On every front, the wheels were turning to get things moving. Every step was a calculated risk, and each decision represented a possible inflection point in the narrative. They were the dancers, moving in time to the bloody beat of the conflict, which was a ruthless dance that they were performing. However, as the stakes became more significant, so did their determination. They would battle not just for the country that they called home but also for one another. And throughout this difficult time, the ties that they built with one another would be their most powerful weapon.

As word of Emily's discovery spread, the Ukrainian troops in the northeast began to prepare for what they believed to be an impending Russian invasion. They strengthened their defensive fortifications, dug trenches, and distributed ammo as they prepared to defend themselves. The dispersed soldiers quickly reassembled themselves, but this time their joking was replaced with a serious determination. The mood was tight, but there was also a strong sense of solidarity among the individuals; they were prepared to confront whatever challenges came their way.

Emily felt the weight of her finding all the way across the country, in an office that was buried deep within the CIA headquarters. The implications of her research and the weight of duty that came with it were enormous. It was no longer merely a matter of figures and statistics; actual people's lives were on the line. She labored furiously, her eyes locked to her monitors and her fingers working quickly over the keyboard as she combed through every source in search of any scrap of information that would tip the scales in her favor.

Anatoly's mobile gadget alerted him to the arrival of a secret message in the wee hours of the night, when the moon was nowhere in sight. As he read Emily's information, he felt a brief palpitation in his chest. He was aware of the responsibilities he held. He had a fresh resolve, so he went back to his secret operations, but this time he approached them with a feeling of urgency. The next piece of information he obtains could save his life.

Ivan and Yelena were holding their breath as they waited on the northern front's northeastern front. It seemed as if the forest itself had stopped breathing because of the eerie silence that surrounded them. The only thing that broke the quiet was the crackling of their radios and the low-voiced commands that were occasionally given. They were kept warm by their adrenaline despite the freezing cold. They were in an area that was foreign to them, but they did not show any signs of fear. They not only had one another, but also a goal. A purpose that was greater than both of them, and more significant than the worries that they had.

Then, there was a break in the quiet. The low rumble of automobiles could be heard in the distance, and it was getting louder. As the artillery fire began to fall, the darkness of the woodland was suddenly pierced by brilliant bursts of light. It was now the beginning of the Russian attack. Ivan, Yelena, and their other teammates hunched down, their expressions becoming more resolute as a result of their resolve. This was the end. The time that they had been waiting for had finally arrived. The new front had finally started.

The protagonists found themselves in the middle of the mayhem and fighting that broke out during the night as the night progressed. Emily prayed that her research would end up being useful, despite the fact that she was thousands of miles away but yet linked to the conversation through technology. Anatoly, who was operating covertly behind enemy lines, was getting ready to provide crucial intelligence that may swing the outcome. Ivan and Yelena met the oncoming storm head-on with determination brimming from the depths of their souls and the fire in their eyes.

The sound of artillery ripped through the stillness and calm of the woodland, drowning out the peace and quiet. They were no longer just isolated people with their own tales to tell; rather, they were now a component of something far larger, a force that was working together to combat a shared foe. Every one of them did their bit, fought their own battles, and contributed to the overall narrative of the conflict that would eventually be written in stone.

And thus, the chapter of the new front was written into their lives. It was a chapter full of suspense and uncertainty, of bravery and hope. The tide of battle had once more shifted, and everyone had a part to play in the drama that was being played out on the larger arena of the struggle. Their experiences will become the chapters of a history that has not yet been written, as their lives become more intricately entangled than ever before in the web of conflict. The stage was prepared for the battles that were still to come, the triumphs that were still to be achieved, and the costs that were still to be paid. They were propelled ahead into the unpredictability of the future by the reverberations of the past, where their fates were waiting for them.

CHAPTER 9 "IRON CURTAIN"

The piercing eyes of General Volkov flickered with an internal tempest as he stood in his command tent, surrounded by maps and reports of an endless conflict. The fights he had fought in the past had left scars on his face, which he used as a tough mask of serious focus. However, beyond that mask was a tornado of thoughts. Only he understood the price that he was paying for each command that he gave, and only he knew the price that he was paying for each life that was lost on the battlefield. His men held him in awe, and his opponents terrified him.

In the meantime, fires were raging over the countryside of Ukraine. Villages were leveled and turned into muddy battlefields, and the skies were polluted with the smoke remains of dogfights. The valleys resonated with the sound of tanks, and the skies were stained with the smoky remains of dogfights. The once-calm region has been trapped in the grip of a lengthy and menacing shadow created by the prospect of war.

In response to this, the Ukrainian army fought back with unwavering persistence, and they were aided in their efforts by Anatoly and his resistance organization, who provided them with important intelligence. Every retaken hamlet and every successful defense of an assault served as further evidence of their unstoppable will. Their minds were made up, and their emotions were fueled by the belief that they had to defend their country, their families, and their freedom.

Emily's involvement became increasingly important as the intensity of the fight increased. She labored without stopping to put together cryptic knowledge, each tidbit of information representing a potential escape route. Her efforts went beyond the simple fulfillment of a task; rather, they were now motivated by a personal devotion to the individuals who were a part of the conflict.

Nevertheless, the war that was the most significant took place within General Volkov himself. He was divided between doing his duty and following his conscience, being loyal and being moral. Being the son of an officer who had received several decorations, patriotism was his birthright, and devotion was his natural tendency. However, the war had put a shadow over his homeland, making it difficult to differentiate between what was good and what was evil.

He had been trained to obey commands and carry them out without question since he was a soldier. This conditioning, however, started to break down with each new story of civilian losses and each new sight of destroyed houses and lives. Every night, he would lie awake and struggle with the ghosts of his deeds, the cost of his commands, and the weight that each life lost put on his spirit. Despite this, at the crack of morning he would put on his uniform, the medals on his chest serving as a clear reminder of his responsibility.

While he was alone himself, he reflected on the advice that his father had given him many years earlier: "Remember, son, the uniform does not make a man; his actions do." The pull of his father's teachings and his responsibility to his country created a rift inside him that threatened to break him apart as he struggled with these statements.

Consequently, as the fires of war burned over Ukraine, they also raged within General Volkov, influencing his path, his character, and even his very soul. As the conflict's Iron Curtain descended more heavily and more darkly, the stage was set for further fights, other successes, and additional losses, each leaving an indelible imprint on the canvas of this horrible struggle.

For General Volkov, the days passed in a haze of smoke and fire, filled with meetings to discuss strategy and restless nights. During the time that he was orchestrating the massive Russian military machine, he maintained his quiet and kept the storm that was raging inside of him under tight control. In the eyes of his adversaries, he became a person to be feared, and in the eyes of his allies, he became an icon worthy of admiration; yet, the mirror revealed a man who was fighting to reconcile his humanity with the requirements of war.

In the middle of all of this emotional upheaval, a particular order arrived, one that would put the limits of his job, as well as his sense of right and wrong, to the test. His commanders gave the order to launch a full-scale assault on a number of Ukrainian towns and villages that were thought to be hiding members of the resistance. It was decided that the loss of civilian life was a price worth paying.

Back on the Ukrainian side of the border, Anatoly and his gang had taken up residence in one of these villages, where they offered comfort and reassurance to the scared locals. Emily's network was the source of the information that informed them about the upcoming onslaught. They braced themselves, readying themselves to put up a fight against the overwhelming Russian force, which was given to them in advance.

While all was going on, Emily was toiling away in her secluded office in Washington, DC, and she began to feel an increasing feeling of hopelessness. Despite the physical separation, the cost of the battle was deeply ingrained in her heart. Each letter that was intercepted and each satellite image became a spectral reminder of the anguish that was taking place. A feeling of impending doom was spurred on by the report of the upcoming attack. She had friends in those areas; some of them were people she had never met in person but had come to know and appreciate through her job. The general public likes Anatoly.

General Volkov found himself in a perilous position as the Russian forces began to assemble. The command felt heavy in his hands, but the burden it placed on his heart was far greater. He fixed his gaze on his soldiers as they readied themselves for another attack, another day in torment. The spectral depictions of innocent lives that had been taken were prominent in his mind's eye.

The general thought back on his strict upbringing and

remembered his father's severe glare. But he also recalled his mother, her gentle touch, her compassionate gaze, and her unshakeable faith in the inherent goodness of humankind. He had previously been unaware of how he had allowed one aspect of his upbringing to overwhelm the other aspects of his upbringing. He was now aware of the inconsistency in his thoughts and his choices. The revelation smacked him in the face like a punch.

General Volkov was confronted with a decision that would have repercussions not just for himself but also for the course of the war and the lives of many others. This option would determine the outcome of the conflict and the lives of countless others. In the midst of all of this chaos, the general's emotions battled with his sense of duty as a soldier, which helped set the stage for an exciting finale.

The time has come to act. From his position in the command post, General Volkov observed the lights of the armored vehicles as they flashed in the twilight. The soldiers, which appeared to be nothing more than specks from this vantage point, moved around like gears in a massive war machine, each contributing to the imminent assault. The peace that prevailed despite the impending calamity was only a false sense of security brought on by the thick blanket of stillness that covered the playing field.

In the quiet of his rooms, Volkov struggled to make sense of the internal turmoil he was experiencing. The words of his father kept playing over and over in his head: "We do what we must for our motherland." But he couldn't get his mother's voice out of his head. It was calmer than usual, but it was determined as she said, "Every life is precious, and every soul carries a piece of the divine."

During this time, Anatoly and his crew were preparing the residents of the Ukrainian hamlet that was under danger by preparing them for the worst-case scenario. The holy cross was casting long shadows in the dim lighting, transforming the church in the village into a temporary castle. Everyone, including women, men, and even children, had a look of equal parts dread and determination in their eyes as they prepared to maintain their position. The presence of death was palpable, but so was an air of defiance in the air as well.

Emily sat in the gloomy glow of her computer screen in Washington, District of Columbia, with her pulse thumping rapidly as she followed the motions on the screen. She felt helpless, like a bystander who had no choice but to watch a disaster unfold from a distance of thousands of miles. She made a small prayer as she pushed her fingertips to the glass and said the words.

The Russian onslaught started just as the first rays of dawn started to illuminate the sky. The peace and quiet of the early morning were disrupted by the din of the tanks, the screech of the jet engines, and the clamor of the conflict. However, despite being subjected to such a barrage, the community held its ground. The villagers were roused by Anatoly, who led the attack while wearing a mask to conceal his features. They responded to the Russian assault with a barrage of homemade explosives, which transformed the peaceful morning into a blazing display of resistance.

Volkov was stationed at his command post when the chaos broke out, and as he watched everything unfold, his heart sank with each cloud of smoke that ascended into the early sky. The weight of knowing that this victory had come at the expense of the lives of innocent people was one that he would have to bear for the rest of his life. The words of his father were like a chilly echo, while the words of his mother were like a sad lament.

He settled on a choice as a result of his strengthened commitment. He would be in charge of this attack, but he would also work to find a means to reduce the casualties and the amount of damage done. He would do this dangerous task for the honor of his homeland, in remembrance of his deceased mother, and in the pursuit of atonement.

Emily was able to see the Russian invasion from her secluded vantage point, where she discovered an intriguing pattern. Their approaches were foreseeable, and their pattern of assault was almost deliberate; it was almost as if someone was attempting to communicate via the mayhem of the conflict. She had a wacky idea pop into her head. Is there a possible clue here? A lead that may be used by the defenders? Behind the impenetrable barrier that was the Iron Curtain, the germ of an audacious scheme began to take root.

In the middle of the mayhem and conflict, Anatoly was engaged in a battle not only against the invading forces but also with himself. He clenched his hand around a locket that had a fading photo of Oksana, his late wife. In sharp contrast to the unrelenting nature of the reality that was pressing down on him, her gentle smile appeared to float on the sepia tones of the snapshot. Each shell that detonated and each person that was lost filled him with a chilling resolve that strengthened his determination. He was no longer fighting only for Ukraine; rather, he was fighting for Oksana, the love they had, and the tranquility they yearned for together.

Emily, in the meantime, started to record the offensive patterns she had seen while her eyes were bloodshot and her focus was unshakable. Her hands glided skillfully across the keyboard as if they had a life of their own, charting out each movement and every strategic decision. She was on to something, despite the mind-numbing intricacy of the situation. There was a possibility of making progress. It was as simple as her extending her hand and grabbing hold of it.

At the same time, the Russian general Volkov was engaged in a struggle with his personal demons. He looked down at the map that was spread out in front of him. The vast contours, which were denoted with lines and color codes, symbolized lives: lives that were lost, lives that were rescued, and lives that were eternally altered as a result of the conflict. He focused with an intensity on the map that belied the anguish going on inside of him. Even though his orders were crystal clear, his conscience, which was riddled with uncertainty and sorrow, questioned every action.

The moment had come for Volkov to choose on a choice. This is a dangerous action, one that has the potential to put his soldiers in harm's way; nevertheless, if it were to be carried out flawlessly, it would speed up the attack and reduce the number of civilian losses. He had no idea if his bosses would agree with him or if it would even be successful, but he felt obligated to give it a go anyhow.

When Anatoly returned to the devastated town, he found that Emily had sent him a message in code. While his heart was racing, he was able to decipher the message. It consisted of only a time and a set of coordinates, nothing more and nothing less. But for Anatoly, it was the difference between life and death; it was a ray of light in the midst of the darkness. His voice could be heard over the chaos of the battle as he rallied his misfit group of soldiers. In the event that this was their final chance, they would make the most of it.

Both parties, as the day wore on into the evening, made preparations for what was ahead. Emily, who was located many thousand miles away, could only wait and keep her fingers crossed. The future of the hamlet, the outcome of Volkov's daring gamble, and the course of events to come in the fight all hung perilously in the balance on the blade of the knife.

The town transformed into a stage where the drama of life and death would soon be played out as twilight began to sink in and blanket the area in its melancholy colors. The strange silence was sporadically disrupted by the distant booms of artillery, which sounded like a terrifying symphony playing to the rhythm of terror. The warriors, a mishmash of tenacity and despondency, had their heads muddled by the concept of the inevitability of the situation, but their hearts were filled with courage.

Anatoly turned his attention for the very last time to the photograph of his cherished Oksana. When he realized that his life had gone full circle, he let out a giggle that was devoid of any mirth. As he had promised her, he was at this location to safeguard his property. He looked around at the faces of his allies and saw the same dogged resolve reflected in their eyes. Before he tucked the locket away and mentally prepared himself for what was to come, he said a prayer in his brain and made a promise to Oksana once again.

While this was going on, Emily was focused on the brilliant computer screen in the dimly lit room while she clenched her teeth and bit down hard on her bottom lip thousands of miles away. The most recent Ukrainian locations were displayed on the computerized map of the battlefront as red dots. These dots represented the heartbeats of men and women who were fighting a war they were destined to lose. She was aware of the sacrifices that had been made and those that were still to come. She sent another batch of encoded information to Anatoly by clicking her mouse and transmitting it to him. She had high hopes that each click would help someone survive.

General Volkov, on the other hand, was seen standing erect in his command center as he struggled with the ethical conundrum that was raging within of him. The reality of pointless killing stained the zeal of nationalism, which had hitherto been untarnished. His instructions were quite clear: wipe out the competition. However, his heart longed for a different course, one that resulted in the fewest number of victims possible. He issued the instructions in a covert act of defiance, which was a strategic action that had the potential to save lives but would also disclose his position to the adversary. He risked his reputation, his career, and the lives of his men by taking the gamble.

Anatoly, who was back in the hamlet, received the encoded message that Emily had sent, and he deciphered it while his hands were shaking. It was an idea that was bold and maybe dangerous, but it carried some promise. It was a strategy that placed their hopes squarely on the chest of their adversary. In order to rally his men and inspire them, Anatoly said words that held the weight of their independence. They readied themselves with a renewed sense of determination, getting ready to draw the line and maintain their position.

The anxiety increased with every passing second, as the drumbeat of conflict became ever more audible. Emily was helpless beyond the scope of her position as she waited with bated breath thousands of miles away. She sat there and watched as the frontline soldiers moved around the computerized map in accordance with her intelligence. Even General Volkov stood back and watched as his troops disobeyed instructions from higher up and forged their own way forward.

The stage was prepared for action beneath the dark canopy of the night sky, with the only light coming from the flashes of explosions in the distance. The protagonists had been established, and their respective roles were crystal obvious. The dramatic conclusion to this epic narrative of conflict was almost here, and the stage was about to be set for its beginning.

Emily first became aware of what was going on when the digital dots on her map started to move, establishing a pattern of assault that was unlike anything else she had ever witnessed. General Volkov was disobeying his instructions and working to reduce the number of deaths among the Ukrainian forces. She felt a glimmer of hope begin to stir inside her chest. If she had the ability to guess his approach, they would have a better chance of minimizing their losses.

Her hands were moving quickly over the keyboard as she scanned the many screens in front of her, which displayed satellite images, heat maps, and terrain analyses. She was painting a picture of the battlefield for Anatoly. It was a picture that had the promise of triumph, even if it was painted with the sad colors of sacrifice.

Volkov stood still in the icy command center, staring at the charts as his eyes hunted for gaps in the plan. He was looking for any chance he could get to save his soldiers. A radio in the far corner of the room began to make staticky noises as it powered up, and the monotone voice of an underling reporting the progress of his soldiers reverberated around the tense chamber. The execution of his plan had begun, and as a consequence, the lives of his warriors hung in the balance. His stomach was in knots from the icy dread that he felt, but he told himself that this was for the greater good.

After returning to the devastated village, Anatoly briefed his soldiers on the counterattack strategy that was based on Emily's intelligence. A ray of optimism shined through in each of their eyes despite the bleakness of the situation. They were aware of the cost of this conflict and realized that they were the only thing that stood between their nation and the invading armies. However, they were also aware that each of them had a part to play in the bigger story of freedom and survival that was being told.

The duration of the lull before the storm was excruciatingly drawn out, serving as a terrible reminder of the carnage that was still to come. The moon, a spectator in silence, produced long shadows that moved gracefully in sync with the flickering light from a fire that was not far away. The sound of the cracking was a sharp contrast to the faint hum of the enemy tanks in the distance, which were the mechanical animals that threatened to crush their hopes of freedom.

Then, in the wee hours of the morning, it started to happen. After being enveloped in a foreboding stillness for a brief period of time, the settlement suddenly exploded in a cacophony of gunfire and artillery bursts. Emily's pulse was racing in her chest as she watched the mayhem play out on the televisions in her room. General Volkov was stationed in the command center where he heard the initial reports of the confrontation. His expression was one of stoic resolve as he did so. On the battlefield, Anatoly and his troops stood their position, despite the barrage of incoming enemy fire and the onslaught of approaching foe forces. They were like an iron curtain that never wavered in its resolve.

The night had not yet come to an end, and the shadow puppets of battle was still performing on the stage, with each movement carving a story of bravery and selflessness. It was a dance of survival and defiance, a dance that would continue until the dawn delivered a new day and with it, a new hope. This dance would continue until the morning offered a new day and with it, a new hope. The stage was still empty when the lights went off. The most exciting part of the story was still to come.

A fatigued Volkov prepared himself mentally for the reports that were about to arrive as dawn began to appear in the distance. He was aware that his directions had not been followed. They had fought the adversary far sooner than had been expected, which resulted in casualties among the adversary's troops. He took off his spectacles and rubbed the bridge of his nose as he took a minute to collect his thoughts before confronting the brutal truths of battle. His acts were not motivated by disloyalty to his country of origin; in fact, just the reverse was true. He was dedicated to the lives of his soldiers and faithful to a feeling of humanity that was rapidly fading in the face of merciless methods and the cold calculations of war. He was committed to the cause of mankind.

Emily watched as the computerized representations of human lives manipulated and collapsed on the screen in the CIA headquarters where she was. The lines on her chart portrayed a narrative of suffering and sacrifice, as valiant men gave their lives while others stepped forward to fill their shoes. As the events transpired, it broke her heart, but she persisted in her job, keeping her hands steady and her thoughts focused. Every tidbit of information and every pattern that was uncovered had the potential to be the deciding factor in whether or not the guys who were on the ground would survive.

Anatoly moved on despite the fact that everything around him was in disarray. On the battlefield, smoke and debris obscured the view, and the pungent odor of explosives lingered in the air. His heart was pounding in his chest as he walked from cover to cover, directing his troops, and making hasty choices that may change the course of their lives with a cool head that belied the anguish going on inside him. His soldiers, who looked to him for leadership, imitated his actions while maintaining expressions of grim resolve on their faces.

The loud melody of conflict reverberated through the streets of the village. Homes that were previously teeming with activity now lay in ruins and are being used by the military as makeshift shields. Anatoly caught a glimpse of a nearby church, which had suffered damage to its once-spotless front, including fires and gunshot holes. However, the golden cross that stood atop the structure was illuminated by the first rays of sunlight as the day broke. He never let go of the picture because it represented for him resiliency and optimism in the face of adversity.

On the other side of the battlefield, a young Russian soldier who had just barely left his teens could be seen shaking as he reloaded his pistol. Fear was written all over his face, but so was determination. It was said among the ranks that General Volkov had disobeyed orders, and when he did, it filled him with a sense of pride and made him feel like he was a part of something more meaningful than a mindless war machine. It inspired him to fight even harder. The viciousness of his volleys forced Anatoly's soldiers to take a step back, which shifted the position of the battlefield.

Emily analyzed the new patterns and then informed Anatoly of this shift in her findings. As the Ukrainian took in the new information, his eyes became narrower. They were forced to put up a fight. In spite of the tiredness that was beginning to seep into his bones, he was able to keep his voice strong and steady as he rallied his soldiers. They would not be stifled with beatings or silenced in any way. They were implacable and unrelenting, much like the Iron Curtain.

The conflict continued unabated even as the dawn began to rise, producing elongated shadows and bathing the devastated town in a warm, golden light. The dance of survival had by no means come to an end. New heroes were born in the furnace of battle with each passing second, and every heartbeat reflected the resounding determination to fight, to survive, and to defend. They were the watchmen over their land, and they would defend it right up until the moment they took their last breath, right up until the very end.

As Volkov opened the encrypted report, his hands began to quiver, and his eyes widened as he saw the figures of those who had been killed. He muttered an expletive under his breath while pounding his fist on the table. His thoughts immediately went back to the orders that had been issued to him, orders that, had he executed them, would have resulted in an even larger body count. His mind raced. He was split between doing his job and being human, between being loyal to Russia and to his soldiers. As he contemplated his options, which were all inherently risky and might either bring him success or bring him ruin, his chest began to feel heavy.

Unexpectedly, a light shed some illumination on his musings. On the battlefield, the young Russian soldier was not classified as being among the dead but rather among the wounded. Volkov let out a sigh of relief as he discovered a ray of hope amidst the misery. This was a fight to the death, a grueling competition in which the victor was determined not by who won the most games but rather by who lost the fewest. He was aware that it was impossible for him to stop all of the casualties, but he could at least try to reduce their number.

While this was going on, Emily was attempting to anticipate the next move that the enemy would make while tracing her finger over the shifting front lines on her digital map. Her pulse was beating. Her screen was flooded with reports of slain warriors, and each one was like a knife in her heart. She continued on, her thoughts turning into a tactical chessboard as she attempted to negotiate the intricate and ever-changing patterns of the war. She was determined.

Her focus was broken when she received an unexpected call from Anatoly. He wanted a study of the most recent actions taken by the Russian government. His voice was worn out, tainted with the toll of conflict and grief, yet below it all was a steely determination that Emily found to be inspiring. She indicated with a nod that she would transmit the findings as quickly as she could.

As soon as Anatoly finished his call, the combat resumed with a vengeance. He could see the enemy's determination beginning to falter. His own weary but resolute soldiers quickly took advantage of the situation. They pressed forward, regaining the valuable territory that they had previously lost, in response to a rousing call. He felt a revitalized feeling of optimism when he saw the Ukrainian flag flying over the community for the second time in as many days.

As they proceeded onward, Anatoly could feel a pounding in his chest caused by his heart. His attention was drawn to the broken church with the golden cross that, despite the mayhem, was still able to capture the light of the sun. He found himself saying a prayer in his head, a secret request for his soldiers to have the will to persevere. His thoughts strayed to his family, the images of their faces becoming hazy in the midst of the smoke and dust that permeated the room. Every action he made was for them; every shot he fired was for their protection; and every life he ended was an unfortunate but unavoidable consequence of the road he traveled.

The young Russian soldier continued to fight despite having his arm bandaged and his face contorted with anguish. The ranks were strengthened by the rumors that had arisen about Volkov's disobedience, which had spread throughout the ranks. They battled not for a nameless state but for a man who knew their terror and their need to live. This gave them the motivation to fight. He cast a quick glance toward the sun just beginning to rise, a sign of a fresh start and of optimism. Even though the threat of death was hanging over the battlefield, he was going to fight for that dream nevertheless.

The din of the conflict was a never-ending tempest, accentuated by the deafening rattling of gunfire, the piercing rattle of artillery, and the shouts of soldiers engaged in the rough dance of warfare. Volkov observed resolutely as his soldiers maintained their position, his gaze harsh and unwavering. He was acutely aware of the gravity of their confidence in him, and he carried the duty that came along with it with a resolute sense of fortitude. It was because to his commands that men were put in danger of being killed, but it was also due to his orders that people's lives may be spared.

His attention was drawn to the picture of his wife and children that was tucked away in the bottom right-hand corner of his map. The memories of their joy and love served as a soothing salve against the mayhem that was all around them. He battled for them, for the future they had ahead of them. Even though he was aware that not all of his men would make it back, he was adamant that they all be given the opportunity to reunite with their families. His instructions were a relic from a time he had desperately sought to leave behind, and the weight of guilt that he carried with him was oppressive.

Emily discovered new insights about the dispute as she dug deeper into her investigation and realized that the conflict's rhythm revealed patterns. The ebb and flow of forces, the unexpected retreats, and the stubborn pushes all painted the picture of a leader who was torn between his job and his conscience. She was familiar with the price of such a fight since she had experienced it on her own when she joined the CIA. She paid close attention to Volkov's behaviors, tracking his every move in an effort to divine his next move and unravel the mystery that was hiding behind the man's behavior.

Anatoly, in the meantime, was standing smack dab in the middle of the uproar, his heart beating out of his chest like a battle drum. Each bullet that whizzed by him served as a jarring reminder of the razor's edge that separated him from certain death. He recalled his wife and the assurance he had given her that he would find his way back to her. He thought about his children, the beaming grins of which served as a lighthouse for him as he navigated this tempest of steel and fire.

Despite the anxiety and the disarray, Anatoly was able to discover a calm inside himself. This was his responsibility; this was his goal. He battled not for the politicians, but rather for the people of Ukraine and for the country of Ukraine. He thought of his fellow soldiers, both men and women, who shared his determination and whose spirits were unshaken despite the scars of combat that covered their bodies. In the middle of the gloomy realities of war, their fortitude shone like a light of hope because it was a demonstration of their character.

The young Russian soldier, whose body was suffering from exhaustion and anguish, glanced up at the sky, which was a canvas of scarlet and gold as the sun was sinking. His eyes shifted to the figure of Volkov, his leader, which stood out like a hulking iron statue against the blazing horizon. They were beginning to feel a glimmer of hope in their hearts as the whispered stories of rebellion went across the ranks. They were not only the implements of war; rather, they were individuals battling for their lives and the lives of their families. The notion gave him new energy, and his determination became as strong as the steely determination of his boss.

In spite of all the atrocities that were committed, there were still instances of humanity that surfaced during times of war. Even while the world around them was engulfed in flames, the people's will to persevere was unshaken, and their determination became as steely as it was tempered in the heat of battle. Every single soldier, every single commander, and every single analyst did their job, and the acts they took wove together to form a complicated tapestry of duty, sacrifice, and survival.

Volkov was in charge of directing the bloody dance of war that was taking place in the conflict's heart, which featured the intertwining of chaos and order as they were being orchestrated. The line was maintained against the attack by his soldiers, who were disciplined and whose wills were steeled and whose eyes were steadfast. The constant background noise of conflict consisted of the rumble of armored vehicles, the boom of artillery, and the deafening clatter of machine guns. Nevertheless, despite the cacophony of devastation, there was a somber solidarity, a mutual comprehension of responsibility and the need for self-sacrifice.

Emily found herself entangled in a complex web of data and intelligence reports when she returned to the boundaries of her workplace. On her desk were scattered intercepted conversations, images of important persons and locations, and maps that had been marked with a variety of colored pins. The information gathered pointed to a struggle that was more complex than simple territorial aggression. The enemy's attacks and withdrawals followed a predictable pattern that had an interesting rhythm to it. It appeared as though someone was just gaining time by delaying. The revelation was like being shocked by electricity. She was obligated to pass along this knowledge since it had the potential to alter the course of the game.

While fighting in the trenches, Anatoly found himself in the middle of a conflict between life and death. The trenches were like horrible cemeteries, yet they were also the place where bravery and fraternity were born. He had witnessed men die; their features being seared indelibly into his mind. But he also witnessed a fraternity that was built out of difficulties faced together, relationships that were made in the heat of combat. They were the sons and daughters of Ukraine, steadfast in spirit while bearing the wounds of battle on their bodies. Every triumph, regardless of how seemingly little they were, fueled optimism. Every setback served to strengthen their determination.

This reality of violence might be seen reflected in the eyes of the young Russian solider, Misha. He was a conscript who had been torn from his peaceful existence and thrust into the chaos of war. Fear was an ever-present companion, but so was the steadily expanding conviction that he was a part of something greater than himself, than Volkov, and even than the conflict itself. Each day, he mustered the fortitude to keep going and fight, propelled by the image of the silhouette of his captain, which represented defiance against the mechanization of war.

The haze of battle acted as an enveloping cloak that masked the reality of the situation and amplified the sense of dread. However, despite all, mankind managed to keep going. In the middle of the muck, blood, and gunpowder, there was bravery, sacrifice, and an unyielding resolve to save what they held most dear. These were conflicts for more than just territory; they were fighting for their history, for their lives in the present, and for the possibility of a peaceful future.

The news of the recent victory achieved by the Ukrainians was met with resentment and disappointment in Moscow. The highest level of command was called together for a last-minute emergency meeting. The clamorous voices reverberated throughout the elegant rooms, and the maps that were laid out on the long table appeared to mock the speakers. Volkov, on the other hand, stood out due to his lack of speech.

The Russian general's intellect was torn between doing the right thing and following his conscience, and his heart was caught in the vice of pain. He stayed quiet as the rapid-fire exchange of tactics and retaliatory measures, as well as the impending preparations for escalation, were discussed. His instructions were quite clear: complete obedience with no room for doubts. But despite this, there was a growing sense that something wasn't quite right. Because he was a soldier and an instrument of his country's desire, he was required to repress his own feelings; after all, he was a soldier. But what happens when the will of the country diverges from the route that mankind should take? What are the repercussions of disobedience, and what are the benefits of adhering to the rules?

When they got back to the Ukrainian front, the bone-chilling cold served as a daily reminder of how difficult their position actually was. The soldiers had begun to construct improvised shelters so that they could protect themselves from the piercing winds. His heart filled with pride as Anatoly saw his soldiers battle the elements with the same tenacity and determination with which they battled their opponents. In spite of the subzero conditions, the morale of his guys was like a blazing blaze, flashing with moments of pleasure and laughter among the gloomy reality they were facing.

Emily was in Washington, and she was sitting at her desk with her shoulders down and her eyes bloodshot from reading numerous pages of reports and intelligence briefings. She had been seeking for this lead for quite some time, and she had finally located it in the form of a series of encoded signals that had been transmitted between Russian military and an unknown receiver. It was a puzzle, a possible Achilles heel for the opposing armies, and it was a mystery. She was well aware that this had the potential to be a decisive factor in their favor.

Misha was engaged in his own conflict on the Russian side of the conflict. The seed of an audacious concept, a non-violent resistance, was sown in his head at a meeting that took place in secret with a few of other troops who shared his worldview. But was there really a chance of such happening amidst the relentless clatter of guns and the constant downpour of artillery fire?

As a result, the battlefield was a pulsating hub of secret agendas, last-ditch plans, and the uncompromising will of its performers. The iron barrier was not merely a geopolitical split; it was also a fight within each of these individuals. They were stuck between their history and the emerging present, and they were teetering on the verge of a future that was unknown to them.

As the sun went down over the devastated landscapes, an iron veil of darkness descended, symbolizing the unbreakable split between the countries involved in this fight as well as the division that exists inside the hearts of those who are involved. In Moscow, General Volkov was seen sitting in his lavish office with the sole light coming from a single candle, which cast a shadow over his face. His thoughts kept going back to the heated discussions that had taken place earlier in the day, the horrifying accounts of loss, and the faces of his own soldiers whose lives had been sacrificed for the cause. He closed his eyes and said a prayer in his head, pleading for wisdom in the midst of the moral upheaval he was experiencing.

Emily's workplace in Washington, DC, was a jumble of deciphered communications and reams of maps. As she finally deciphered the obscure Russian signal, a gleam of triumph lit up her bleary eyes. She felt like a champion. She did not waste any time in reporting her findings to her superiors since she was aware that they would affect the way the war was being fought. She was unable to stop herself from thinking about the people whose lives were represented by the pieces of paper as she switched out the lights and left the relics of her efforts scattered around her desk. As she went out into the chilly night air, the notion was sobering, and it was one that combined with the sense of achievement she was feeling.

Anatoly's face was lighted by the flames of a makeshift bonfire that had been constructed on the Ukrainian front. He sat with his troops, the sound of their unyielding spirit resonating throughout the night in the laughter that they shared. Each guy had his own history, his own purpose for being there, and his own shadows that danced in the embers of the fire as the light from the fire flickered. They were more than simply warriors fighting on a battlefield; rather, they were the manifestation of their nation's unrelenting resiliency and its invincible spirit.

Misha's clandestine gathering, which had been taking place in a remote part of the Russian camp, broke up as night fell, their mutterings of defiance blending in with the sounds of the night. In the meantime, the Russians continued to advance. The germ of disobedience had been planted, and it was being fed by their mutual displeasure as well as their growing optimism for a peaceful settlement to the conflict.

Each of our characters' levels of confidence, hesitation, and resolution increased as the night wore on, mirroring the progression of the night itself. Every one of them, in their own unique manner, was getting drawn further into the vicious mouth of the conflict. They were becoming ensnared in its web. But despite the dense iron curtain of strife and upheaval, glimmers of humanity started to show through. These glimmers of humanity were fragile but resilient, and they were found in the shadows of the past and the promise of the unknown   future.

CHAPTER 10 "RETRIBUTION"

At the same time as the early morning mist clung low to the earth, concealing the footfall of the Ukrainian forces that were advancing, the atmosphere was electric with expectancy. Soldiers crept stealthily like shadows, their pulses beating in time with the tense pulsing tension that seized the contested regions.

There was also Anatoly, who had a serious expression on his face and appeared to be quite determined. His thoughts were filled with recollections of slain companions, and he could also hear the eerie, far-off echo of the church bell in his village. The constant reminders of what he had lost served to strengthen his resolve. He wasn't only fighting for the liberation of Ukraine at this point; he was fighting for vengeance as well.

General Volkov, who was stationed in a strongly guarded Russian command post, was staring at the map at the same time. He was acutely aware of the quickly altering dynamics. His directives were quite clear: Hold the line at all cost, despite the fact that they were tough to stomach. Despite this, his attention kept wandering to the northeast, towards Belarus. He thought back to the fervent young warrior he had talked to, a person who exemplified the spirit of resistance that he had previously respected and maybe still did. He recalled meeting this kid.

Misha was plotting his most audacious mission to date several hundred kilometers away in a sleepy village in Belarus, which was guarded by a monument of Lenin depicted as having a serious expression on its face. It was a policy that was fraught with peril, one that would either halt the progress the Russians had made or result in the rapid and ruthless retaliation of the Russians.

His strategy was straightforward yet nonetheless daring. Misha had a plan to destroy the primary artery of gasoline and ammunition that supplied the advancing Russian divisions, and he planned to do so by utilizing his knowledge of the Russian supply routes. If it were effective, it would not only halt the advance of the Russian forces but also provide Ukraine with the much-needed break to reorganize and prepare for a counteroffensive.

The faint glow of portable lanterns created long, swirling shadows about Misha and his team as they loaded the few surviving trucks with improvised explosives. The anxiety was apparent as they worked. Each guy was aware of the significance of their mission and the fact that it was a distinct potential that they might not survive it. Battle had left its mark on their features, and it showed in the ferocious resolve that was etched on them. They weren't just engaged in a battle; rather, they were taking on a monster in order to win back their independence.

As morning neared, the countryside once more morphed into a battlefield in preparation for the day ahead. Under the rising light, the tenacity and bravery of the Ukrainian soldiers did not waver as they continued to press their advantage. In Belarus, Misha's gang proceeded covertly while their hearts were thumping with excitement and their thoughts were silently praying for the accomplishment of their goal.

The ghosts of previous conflicts and the impending shadow of vengeance cast a gloomy yet resilient image of the Eastern European theater as they hung like a shroud over the dawn. The conflict was by no means done; rather, it had just moved into a new and more dangerous phase. After all, individuals who want justice can be just as likely to wield the sword of retribution as those who are determined to keep their iron grasp on power. Retribution is a sword with a double-edged blade.

In the wee hours of the morning, the Ukrainian onslaught seemed like a ghost moving through the darkness as it advanced. The rumbling of tanks could be heard as their hulking metal bodies snaked between the structures, kicking up muck in their wake. Artillery crews toiled with their imposing machines while the booming retort of their guns was muted by the deep fog that covered the battlefield. Anatoly found himself in the commanding position of a squadron. His heart was thumping against his ribcage, but the icy steel of his weapon provided a somber sense of solace.

As they made their way forward, they unexpectedly came across what appeared to be an abandoned Russian position. Amidst the chaos, there were heaps of empty cartridges, chilly fire pits, and ration cans that had been hurriedly thrown. As Anatoly gave the order for his troops to search the area, a heavy sense of unease pervaded the atmosphere. In the middle of the eerie calm, there was suddenly a click that reverberated around the room. It turned out to be a tripwire and a trap. The ground was jolted as a result of the explosion, which was followed by a catastrophic shockwave that tore through their ranks.

While everything was going on, Misha, a Belarusian warrior, and his guys were racing towards the Russian supply line in their explosive-laden cars. The roads were perilous since they were both slippery from the dew that had fallen overnight and littered with potholes. Misha's knuckles turned white as he clenched the steering wheel tightly in his hands. His heart was beating so hard that it felt like a war drum against his chest. In contrast to the relative quiet of the night, both the odor of gasoline and the sound of the engine of the car sounded unusually loud.

As they got closer to the supply line, they could make out the silhouettes of Russian vehicles against the horizon. They could also hear the clattering of metal and the roar of engines coming closer to them on the breeze of the night. Even though Misha's heart was beating faster, he was unwavering in his determination. He reflected over his house, his loved ones, and his friends, all of whom had been murdered by the intruder. Because he had work to do, he clenched his hands more tightly around the driving wheel.

General Volkov, who was stationed at the Russian command post, was the one who received the news of the Ukrainian advance and the ambush. He did not speak a word while he listened, his serious countenance lit up by the dim light emitted by the command center's many screens. His heart fell as the news continued to pour in, but his demeanor remained stony and unreadable the whole time. He spoke with a harsh, labored tone in an effort to conceal the growing disquiet that was developing within of him and issued counterorders. Even though the consequences of his choices were pressing hard on his shoulders, he was obligated to carry out his responsibilities.

It was not known to the Russian soldiers that they were about to receive the most devastating blow. Misha, who was now within striking distance of his objective, inhaled deeply while silently reciting a prayer to himself. "For Belarus. "For freedom," he whispered under his breath as he detonated the explosives, turning the Russian supply line into a blazing wreck, and lighting up the night sky. The tremors caused by the earthquake rocked the ground under them, creating a terrifying silhouette against the backdrop of the night sky.

The night was filled with acts of vengeance, and the morning forecasted a fight to the death that would be decided by strength of will. The resolute efforts of those who sought justice caused the iron curtain to tremble, but the price was great, and the toll it took on the hearts and souls of those who were engaged was incalculable.

Smoke and dust were seen billowing from the burnt remains of the Russian supply line as the aftermath of the battle lingered heavily in the air. Misha was only a few yards away as he stood there watching the blaze with a sorrowful yet stubborn heart. His crew, who were all just as amazed by the successful surgery they had just completed, started cheering. But Misha did not experience any delight; rather, she felt a sense of empty contentment. This was just one engagement in a much larger conflict.

In the aftermath of the ambush, Ukrainian soldiers found themselves reorganizing their positions across the battlefield. As first responders rushed about trying to treat those who had been hurt, the air was filled with screams for assistance and groans of agony. Anatoly, with dirt and mud streaking across his face, was crouching next to one of his fallen soldiers. He had his hands placed to a wound, and blood was dripping through his fingers.

In spite of the shock and the pain, Anatoly's eyes did not waver in their determination. He shouted for help while keeping his eyes fixed on the young soldier's face the entire time. They were fighting for their country, their independence, and their lives, and the savagery of this combat served as a harsh reminder of why they were fighting.

Not only did he tighten his hold on the injured guy, but he also strengthened his desire to see this fight through to its conclusion.

Back in the command center, General Volkov was having a difficult time processing the information about the severely damaged supply line. Slowly but surely, he was able to piece together the blueprints of the Ukrainian approach, which turned out to be far more sophisticated than he had imagined. He was shaken to his core by the extent of their resiliency and perseverance. In spite of the fact that his adversaries were fellow countrymen, he could not help but respect their energy and their bravery.

Volkov experienced a peculiar feeling despite the fact that the room around him was buzzing with activity. It was as if he were watching a storm approach while perched on the edge of a cliff. He had devoted his entire life to serving his nation and doing what was right. However, he couldn't shake the pictures of the destroyed villages, the dead troops, and the numerous lives of innocent people that were taken. The relentless, heartless, and expensive nature of the conflict was mirrored in his icy, slate-gray eyes, just as it was on the battlefield.

The final act of the chapter of revenge was being acted out to the soundtrack of war cries, the sound of flying bullets, and screams that tore at the heart. It was an echo from the past, an echo that rang through the hearts of the men and women fighting on the battlefield and those working behind enemy lines. The human spirit managed to persevere in spite of the widespread loss of life and widespread damage because it was driven by a desire for freedom, sovereignty, and justice.

As morning got closer, the sun sent a flaming orange and a somber blue glow across the sky. The wreckage from the previous night formed long, dark shadows that seemed to be symbolic of the conflict itself. This darkness was difficult for the first light of morning to dispel since it seemed to be symbolic of the war itself. The dawn of a new day brought with it not the hope of peace, but rather the certainty that fighting would go on throughout the day. The wave of vengeance was becoming stronger, and it appeared like it was going to crest once more as soon as the sun came up.

Misha found himself in the position of being in charge of a new endeavor just as the sun began to rise beyond the horizon, casting light on the remains of the operation that had taken place the night before. In his thoughts, as he stood among the smoldering wreckage of the Russian supply line, the beginnings of a bold new strategy began to take shape.

The Belarusian freedom warrior was aware that the disturbance they had made would not continue indefinitely. Russia would bounce back, respond in kind, and reorganize. However, as a result of their operation, they gained some breathing room, which they could utilize to plot their next move. Misha was steadfast as he turned towards his crew, and the fire in his eyes signified an intensified sense of commitment. There was going to be a daring assault on an adversary's arsenal.

On the opposite side of the conflict, the Ukrainians were making progress advancing further into the contested territory. Anatoly, who was still struggling with the effects of the confrontation from the previous night, pushed his troops ahead. They advanced with caution while maintaining a rapid pace, constantly watching the horizon for any indications of the presence of the adversary.

The push was carried out in a very seamless manner. Because they were still in shock from the destruction of their supply route, the Russians put up very little opposition. The Ukrainians were successful in retaking a number of key strategic positions. However, the awareness that there would inevitably be a counterattack dampened the celebrations of their victory.

Michael was putting in a full day's work at the CIA headquarters, sorting through mountains of information. He had unearthed a crucial piece of knowledge concerning the Russian government's military plan, which was now being put to use. Directives were being given, as well as changes to strategy and adjustments to combat plans. The ripples that Michael had started were having an effect on the war machine as each hour went by, causing the wheels to revolve faster and faster.

During this time, General Volkov was involved in a conflict that was entirely his own. The arrival of each new news brought on fresh waves of dread. His conscience was torn apart by the immorality of his directives. He never wavered in his allegiance to his country, but at what price did he do so? The faces of those who had died continued to torment him, their unspoken accusations playing over and over in his thoughts.

During the wee hours of the morning, he found himself in his personal quarters, looking at an old image of himself. In the picture, he was a young and enthusiastic cadet in the Russian army. He was taken aback by the striking disparity between the man in the snapshot and the person he had developed into over the years. The war had a profound effect on him, as it had also had a profound effect on the world around him.

It seemed as if his own reflection in the mirror was making fun of him, its eyes a frigid gray color and full with questions to which he did not have answers. However, he was certain of one thing. The road he was on was paved with molten rock and spilled blood. And he was tethered to it no matter what the circumstances were; he was a prisoner to his uniform and the responsibility that it stood for.

The region fell into a profound hush as the prospect of yet another day of fighting emerged from the shadows. The stillness before the oncoming storm. On the horizon loomed revenge, a punishment that promised to be as ruthless and brutal as the battle itself. revenge was on the horizon. When the first rays of daylight broke through the gloom, it signaled the beginning of the next terrifying act in this play. The stakes had never been higher.

When they arrived back in Belarus, Misha and the other freedom fighters on his team gathered at their secret hideout. As detailed plans were discussed and maps were laid out over tables, the atmosphere in the room became a bustle of whispered whispers and the sound of clinking metal. Misha detailed their upcoming mission, which will be a daring assault on an adversary's arsenal. The objective was to stymie the Russian advance even more by severing a key link in their supply line.

Misha's voice pierced the commotion that was going on in the room as he began his explanation by saying, "The key is to strike quickly and efficiently." His eyes wandered from one of his combatants to the next, taking in the expressions of resolve on each of their features. "Not only are we competing against the Russian army, but also against the passage of time." Precision is absolutely necessary for the accomplishment of this task.

In Ukraine, Anatoly and his troops continued to advance into contested territory while they were there. Anatoly's uneasiness increased with each successful push that he made. He was all too accustomed to the bitter aftertaste of transitory success, the sense of relative peace that it denoted before the oncoming storm. His troops had a positive attitude as a result of the recent successes they had experienced. However, Anatoly was unable to escape the impression that there was imminent danger.

The knowledge that Michael provided in Washington, DC, was beginning to alter the way the war would be fought. The Ukrainian army's strategy for the upcoming conflict needed to be adjusted as a result of his disclosure of Russia's intended military approach. He was now searching through other data in an attempt to locate additional such crucial bits of information. The analyst had the impression that he was participating in a massive game of chess, in which he was attempting to anticipate the movements of the opponent and devise a strategy in response.

During this time, General Volkov was seeing an increase in the turbulence that was occurring within him. He sensed a growing contradiction between his job and the dictates of his conscience with each command that he gave out. He started to have second thoughts about the ethics of his behavior and the never-ending cycle of violence that he was contributing to. Nevertheless, he was fettered by his obligation; his allegiance to his country kept him from breaking free. The General had a restless night filled with internal deliberation and the gathering of a storm as it progressed through the night.

The next morning arrived, bringing with it both the reverberations of the previous night's preparation and the pressure of the day's activities to be carried out. The sense of tranquility that pervaded the area was an illusion that concealed the impending mayhem that was to come. The chessboard was prepared, and the players were waiting expectantly for their turn. A fresh day of fighting started when the sun crested the horizon and entered the sky. They were about to face the day of retribution.

The sun came up over the countryside of Belarus, giving the white ground a scarlet tint as it illuminated the beginning of the day. As Misha and his colleagues prepared themselves, their breath froze over in the brisk morning air as they put their stuff onto the unremarkable vehicles that they utilized for transportation. Misha couldn't help but send up a quiet prayer as the tension became increasingly obvious in the room. With just a quick nod, the drivers fired up the engines, and the convoy sped out into the early hours of the morning.

In the bowels of the armory, Russian troops were nursing mugs of stale coffee while shaking off the morning chill. They were completely unaware of the imminent attack that was about to take place. The clanking of metal and the humming of machinery were the background score to their ordinary lives; the rumble of war was always in the background.

During this time, Anatoly was leading his troops through a maze of little alleyways in Ukraine. The reverberating calm of the early morning was broken only by the steady cadence of their feet on the pavement. Already perched above the roofs, a pair of his scouts kept a sharp lookout for any indications of the presence of the adversary.

Michael, powered by cups of strong coffee, had only gotten a few hours of sleep in Washington. Although his eyes were red and irritated from gazing at many screens, he experienced a surge of exhilaration whenever he discovered a new piece of information. It pertained to a possible weak spot in the Russian defense, a site that, if successfully attacked, had the ability to affect the dynamic of the front line that was advancing.

Misha's convoy was getting closer and closer to the armory as they were in Belarus. They had an ally in the predawn darkness, which provided shelter for them. Misha took a glance around at his squad, which consisted of random members from the community who had been forced into the role of freedom fighters. "It's now or never," he murmured. "It's now or never."

On Anatoly's end, the first rays of morning revealed an abrupt movement just on the edge of his peripheral vision. When he finally understood what it was, it was already too late. They were about to be struck by a rocket-propelled grenade when they saw it tearing across the early sky. He yelled out, "Take cover!" but the explosion muffled out his voice. "Take cover!"

General Volkov, who was stationed in Russia, was the one who was informed about the impending attack on the arsenal. While he was giving commands, his heart was racing, and in the midst of the imminent threat, he briefly forgot about the specter of his uncertainty. His homeland was in danger, and he had no doubt about what his job was.

The chessboard was moved when night gave way to morning and the day began. The pieces moved, clashed, and a chaotic situation developed as a result. Each side was trying to figure out their next move, their fate, and the developing implications of their deeds as the day of vengeance got well under way.

In the midst of the mayhem, Misha and his crew continued to go forward. There was a steady, deafening boom of gunfire, and the sound of bullets whizzing by was mixed together with the screams of those who were being shot at. Misha moved his soldiers forward based on instinct alone, maintaining his composure despite the tremendous maelstrom that was occurring on the battlefield. They had just entered the armory when a hostile shell went off nearby, unleashing a wave of force and dirt in all different directions. The light in Misha's world suddenly went out, but when he opened his eyes again, there was nothing but determination staring back at him.

In the meantime, Anatoly was knocked off his feet as a result of the first shock caused by the RPG's impact. He shook off the ringing in his ears and stood up among the ruins, his gaze darting over his soldiers who were dispersed and confused. He continued to look about. Even though smoke, dust, and debris obscured his view, he persisted in his pursuit. "Get up, guys! Fight!" He roused the troops, his voice cutting through the thick veil.

Michael, still in possession of the vital piece of knowledge, made a beeline for the office of his director in Washington, where he was stationed. As he attempted to anticipate the response and the consequences of what he had learned, his thoughts were racing in every direction. He gave a tap on the door, took a few deep breaths, and then entered the room, the significance of the situation not being lost on him in the least.

The word of the attack on the armory spread quickly through the higher leadership in Russia when it was revealed. In the midst of the confusion and flurry of instructions, General Volkov found himself at a fork in the path. As a soldier, it was his responsibility to follow orders, but as a man, he questioned the ethics of the activities that were being carried out. The seed of uncertainty was sown deeply within him, and it began to gently influence his choices.

When Misha's troops returned to the battlefield, they broke into the armory. The corridors were filled with loud echoes of the alarm, and the air was heavy with the pungent scent of gunpowder and blood. They worked quickly, setting bombs, and their actions were perfectly coordinated with one another according to their training. They were beginning to feel the adrenaline rush as the countdown clock began to tick.

In Ukraine, Anatoly was in charge of leading a counteroffensive, and his troops gave the enemy a ferocious pushback. He fired his weapon, each shot serving as a representation of his disobedience and a demonstration of his determination. He was so close to winning that he could almost taste it, and he was willing to give up everything for it.

Michael sat in Washington and listened to the Director go through his report while he read it. The lack of response was oppressive, but the nod of approval he received at the very end made it all worthwhile. A fresh plan was implemented, one that had the potential to alter the course of the war in a significant way.

In point of fact, retribution was in the process of being carried out as each side fought their respective wars, both internally and outside. On the anvil of this war, the wounds were getting deeper, but so was the resolve, which was helping to forge legends.

Misha was buried up to his thighs in the shadowy underbelly of the armory. Because he had been touching the icy, unforgiving metal of the explosives, his fingers were burned, but the agony was a faraway worry that was dwarfed by the magnitude of their task. As he wired the final charge, he looked around at his crew, who all had serious expressions on their faces and their hands were completely still. In the greater scheme of things, each of them functioned as an essential piece of the jigsaw. This endeavor was about more than just them; it was about the very identity of their country.

Anatoly was in the front of the assault in the north-eastern sector, his shape a snarl of rage against the dreary backdrop of battle. His body was beaten up, but he wore each scratch and bruise like a badge of pride since they were a monument to his dogged determination. His determination became more steadfast with each lost friend, and it morphed into an unshakable force that propelled his soldiers onward.

Michael found himself in the middle of a tornado as he navigated the halls of power in Washington. As he continued to explain his results, astonishment began to spread around the room, and everyone's expression changed to reflect the significance of what he had discovered. He was in the thick of the action, observing the analysts, strategists, and decision-makers as they struggled to come to terms with the new reality. He was well aware that the globe was poised on the verge of experiencing profound shifts.

In Moscow, General Volkov was engaged in his own struggle against an opposing force. He was sitting in his office, his hands tightly gripping a tumbler of vodka in front of him. Even though the vodka burned a trail down his throat, it was not effective in calming the tempest that was building up inside of him. He had spent his whole life serving his country in the military as a soldier, but the crimes that he was expected to ignore or even carry out continued to torment him. In his visions, he saw the faces of the innocent people whose lives were being torn apart by the fighting. His nation was in danger, and he was divided between doing what was right and following his moral compass.

The world waited with bated breath as Misha's group detonated the last of the explosives in the armory, Anatoly's army advanced the front lines, and Michael's intelligence caused Washington to hum with excitement. The conflict was reaching a peak, and its echoes were rippling throughout all of the nations.

Each persona was acting out their role, and the story of their lives was being woven into a larger picture of conflict and vengeance. Their deeds were influencing the path that history would take, and the destinies of nations were intertwined with their own stories. Their histories were colliding with the present, giving rise to a future that was both uncertain and hopeful. The stakes were extremely high, and the hazards were enormous. Despite this, they pushed forward, carrying the weight of the world on their shoulders and being motivated by a potent mixture of duty, honor, and destiny.

Misha's heart was beating so hard in his chest that it sounded like a drum, and the rhythm echoed the seconds that were counting down until the explosion. He gave his teammates a quick glance, and the faces of determination that they wore mirrored back at him. They hoped for the best while being ready for the worst possible outcome. His forehead was beaded with sweat, and the salty beads that fell there irritated his eyes. He quickly brushed them away while maintaining his concentration on the timer's minute-by-minute digital display.

The continuous din of gunfire and artillery fire could be heard off in the distance, creating an eerie and disturbing symphony of mayhem and devastation. also served as a somber reminder of how urgent and risky their mission was, and also served as the setting for this historic endeavor. The detonators were placed, and the outcomes had been decided. After that, there was nothing left to do but hide away and watch the fireworks.

In the meantime, on the northern front, Anatoly was driving his soldiers forward, his gaze becoming as steely as the freezing gusts that blew over the desolate battlefield. His instructions were as unyielding as the winds. His heart pounded like a battle drum, and each pulse was a painful reminder of the territory they'd conquered and the lives they'd lost along the way.

Every bullet that was fired and every slain soldier was a burden on his moral compass. But he endured it with calm fortitude, his resolve forged in the fires of patriotism and tempered by the frigid touch of revenge. He was fighting not only for himself but also for the remembrance of his family, for the destruction of his community, and for a future in which his nation would no longer tremble in the shadow of a dictator.

Michael was a hub of activity in Washington thanks to his being there. The material that he had unearthed was a bombshell, and its shockwaves changed the direction that the conflict would take. The experts swarmed around him, each one equipped with questions, worries, and apprehension. But Michael remained unmoved at the eye of the storm, his concentration unwavering despite the chaos around him. His disclosure was not only a game-changer for the CIA, but it was also a seismic upheaval in the terrain of international affairs.

General Volkov struggled with his demons as he made his way through the shadowy alleyways of Moscow. Every time he signed an order or delivered a directive, he had the uneasy feeling that he was selling off a piece of who he was. The consequences of his actions, as well as the toll that the conflict took in terms of human lives, were a difficult pill to swallow. His heart was weighed down by the load of guilt, yet he was unable to escape the bonds of duty and allegiance that tied him. His passion for his homeland, on the one hand, and the ethics that gnawed at his conscience, on the other, were a source of internal conflict for him.

The echoes of their previous crimes and the actions they were taking at the time interwoven in this symphony of conflict and revenge, which shaped a future that was fraught with uncertainty. The waves of conflict were becoming stronger and were getting ready to smash against the shores of destiny. Nevertheless, unfazed, our protagonists continued to push forward, forging their ways across the turbulent seas of warfare.

The shooting on the northeast front was so intense that it lit up the battlefield like flashing lights in the middle of the night. The conflict was taking place at night. Tracers were seen arcing across the night sky, and the sound of the bullets piercing the chilly air was reminiscent of angry ghosts. Anatoly pushed his soldiers to move ahead while standing upright in the midst of the mayhem and speaking loudly enough for everyone else to hear. The unrelenting nature of this struggle was demonstrated by the fact that his uniform was covered in the filth and blood of dead friends as well as the grime of the battlefield. His spirit clung to the spark of hope that each strenuous stride ahead was one step closer to a more secure future for Ukraine. This kept his heart beating.

Back in Belarus, Misha and his team made their way back to the place where they were supposed to meet, with the weight of the explosives that they had set looming over them like a heavy shadow. As they raced, their breaths appeared to be coming out in sharp puffs in the chilly air, and the snow beneath their feet masked the sound of their footfall. Every passing second was like a time bomb that was ticking away, with each click repeating the promise of a devastating blow to the Russian army's progress.

As the seconds ticked away on the clock, Misha's heart raced in time with the ticking, his pulse sounding like an endless pounding in his ears. As the time for the explosion became closer and closer, the anticipation kept building up, like a stretched wire that was getting closer and closer to snapping. The strain was intolerable, and the stillness and waiting were like a purgatory all by itself.

Michael sat at his desk in the center of Washington, DC, with his fingers racing over the keys of his laptop. The quiet clicking of his fingers provided a striking contrast to the rapid tempo of his heartbeat. The information that he had found was like a labyrinth; each thread led to another revelation, and the significance of each detail became clear to him gradually, like the dawning of a gloomy day. Every new piece of information caused another wave to be created in the geopolitical pond, with the possible repercussions growing in ever-widening concentric rings.

General Volkov was sitting at his desk in the antiseptic and frigid surroundings of his office in Moscow. The cool metal of the pen in his palm was a sharp contrast to the fevered thoughts that were rushing through his mind at the time. His commands, the people whose lives they changed, and the course of the conflict that they dictated all became a burden he had to bear with every breath he took. Each order served as another blow of the hammer in the construction of the wrought-iron curtain that will surround this fight.

Their current actions threw long shadows into the unknown future, and the judgments they made in the present carried with them the reverberations of the choices they had made in the past. As the clock ticked down to zero, the waves of conflict began to rise in preparation for their impending collision with the beaches of destiny. This collision would reshape the contours of the terrain in ways that no one could have predicted. The culmination of their efforts was about to be accomplished, and the echoes of revenge were becoming closer and closer.

When Anatoly was in the heart of the fight, he felt the ground shake violently beneath his feet. The vibrations had a continuous beat, much like the steady pulse of a heartbeat, and each shake became more severe than the previous one. The air was filled with the rumble of motors, and the staccato of the gunfire was accented by the resounding booms of tank rounds. The booming boom of his voice pierced through the clamor of conflict as he exhorted his soldiers to maintain their positions with a rallying cry.

Each shot fired and each grenade that went out in battle was a shout into the emptiness of war, its echoes bearing witness to the unwavering determination of the Ukrainian warriors. Their unyielding will and unwavering determination in the face of adversity shone like a beacon in the middle of the mayhem. Their stubbornness remained unshaken despite the smoke and dust, as well as the traces of fire that adorned the night sky; it was a towering barricade that protected them from the unrelenting attack.

Misha felt his heart pounding in sync with the unrelenting passage of seconds as he watched the countdown clock that was attached to his wrist. He was in the middle of Belarus. Each tick of the clock served as a reminder of the explosion that was about to take place, a crescendo of expectation leading up to the momentous culmination of the event. The stillness of the night was shattered by the sound of the snow gently crunching underfoot, the hushed whispers of the wind as it passed through the skeletons of the trees, and the far-off sounds of battle.

When the clock hit zero, the night became filled with the sound of many explosions simultaneously. The earth trembled as a result of the seismic activity, and the shockwaves traveled across the wintry landscape. The Russian convoy was turned to a twisted mess of metal and flame after being trapped in the middle of the storm. The explosive fury slowed down their march. The reverberations of the explosion broke the stillness of the night with a shout of defiance that reverberated over the frozen plains of Belarus.

Michael's eyes darted over the screen as he sat in Washington, and the lines of text began to merge into a whirlwind of information. The implications of his discoveries were enormous; they provided a shred of reality that had the potential to untangle the complex web of lies that had cloaked this struggle. Each new piece of information was like a drop in an ocean with potentially significant geopolitical repercussions, with vibrations that might be felt all the way to the borders of international relations.

A storm of contention erupted in Moscow as a result of General Volkov. The instructions that he gave, as well as the routes that they carved out in the terrain of the conflict, were a mirror of his conflicted allegiances. The conflict between his sense of responsibility and his sense of morality was raging within him like a raging tempest. His heart was in the midst of its own fight. Each choice was a stroke of the sword, and the repercussions of each action contributed to the construction of the wrought-iron curtain that was his fate.

As the sounds of revenge resounded over the battlefields, the waves of conflict surged, a force that could not be stopped coming into contact with an object that was unmovable in its defiance. The repercussions of their acts had not yet been completely appreciated, but their effect was certain to change the path that this fight would take in ways that nobody could have predicted. The game of war was not even close to being done, the result was still up in the air, and the future was just as uncertain as the course that a bullet would take in a storm.

The audacious move that Misha made had instantaneous effects on the situation. The elimination of the Russian supply convoy was an undeniable triumph; but it also sparked a vicious act of revenge. The Russian government stepped up its offensive against Belarusian insurgent organizations, but the conflict remained far from ended.

During this time, Anatoly and his forces were in Ukraine, seeing the sky to the north-northeast light up as a result of the explosions. Even though they were separated, they were still able to hear the tremors of the earthquake rumbling through the ground under them. This was a seismic confirmation of Misha's courageous act. A momentary surge of joy ran through the ranks of the Ukrainian armed forces. Their friends were delivering blows to the opposition. They were in with a shot of winning.

However, the reprieve only lasted for a brief period of time. The Russians' response was one of excessive violence, and their fury was unleashed like a hammer onto the Ukrainian people. Anatoly, who was in charge of leading the charge, suddenly found himself in the middle of a fierce battle. Each and every waking second was loaded with peril, and each and every choice was a matter of life and death. On the other hand, Anatoly did not show any sign of flinching as he rallied his soldiers and fought back against the assault.

Michael was in the middle of his own fight back in Washington, where he was stationed. He was aware that he had uncovered something very important, a piece of knowledge that had the ability to change how the battle would ultimately play out. He toiled assiduously, establishing the veracity of his results, vetting the data from several angles, and putting the pieces of the jigsaw together with great care. He was aware that he needed to proceed with caution as the shadows cast by bureaucracy loomed over him.

General Volkov was troubled by the ramifications of his commands while he was stationed in the middle of Moscow. He was aware of the operation that Misha had conducted and the destruction that it had caused in its aftermath. His nation was engaged in a bloody conflict, and he was it weapon in the conflict. The weight of duty and remorse pressed heavily on his chest. Despite this, he was conflicted since he felt obligated to continue because of his responsibility to his country and his allegiance to his motherland.

Every one of the characters was caught in the tumultuous crosscurrents of duty and conflict. Even if their acts were highly personal, they were also a part of a broader story, a sweeping drama that was fast playing out on a global stage. They were both the writers and the protagonists in this drama, with the path of their life being intricately connected with the eventual outcomes of countries.

The noises of the conflict were no longer audible as the sun began to set, which resulted in the landscape that had been ripped apart by conflict having long, ominous shadows thrown across it. The fights that had taken place earlier in the day had been vicious and brutal, leaving profound wounds both on the landscape and in the souls of those who had fought.

Back in Ukraine, Anatoly was standing on a hill overlooking the smoldering wreckage of a city that had once been humming with activity. His attention was riveted on the horizon to the north-northeast, where the telltale indicators of Misha's operation could be seen. He was conscious of the fact that he was standing on a brink, both literally and figuratively. The norms of battle and allegiance were being twisted beyond recognition as the world that he knew was falling apart all around him. Despite this, he stayed firm, his resolve honed by the conflicts of the day and bolstered by the conviction that he battled for a purpose that was higher than himself.

Michael sat by himself in his office on the other side of the ocean, transfixed on the now-deciphered paper that was shown on his computer. This was a secret that had the ability to alter the path that the conflict would take. He was well-versed in the art of keeping secrets, but this one was unique. This one held the burden of the lives of countless people as well as the fate of nations that were on the verge of extinction. He drew in a long breath as he prepared himself mentally for the storm that was imminently approaching.

In Moscow, General Volkov was seen standing by himself in his office and gazing out the window at the metropolis that never ceased to be active. His homeland, which appeared to be at peace on the surface, continued to beat despite the conflict that was being fought in its name. In addition to being a soldier and a servant of his nation, he was also a guy who was capable of compassion and who struggled with uncertainty. Duty and morality began to blend together for him as he struggled to determine what part he should play in the unfolding fight.

In the meantime, Misha was making preparations for another operation deep into Belarus. His morale remained unbroken in spite of the Russian government's retribution. His actions had generated a domino effect, and he was aware that the stakes had significantly increased as a result. But for Misha, this wasn't simply a war for independence; it was a fight for survival, for the fundamental essence of what it meant for his nation to be alive.

As a consequence of this, the protagonists of our narrative found themselves perched on the precipice of a chasm just as the story's climax event was taking place. There was still a long way to go in this fight, the stakes were becoming higher, and the waves of revenge were getting stronger. This was their moment of reckoning, and as the lights went out on this eventful day, one thing was certain: the morning would bring fresh conflicts, new difficulties, and new opportunities to influence the path that history would take.

EPILOGUE: "THE LONG SHADOW"

After three years, the globe had undergone a transformation that was unrecognizably similar to the seismic upheaval that the conflict had produced. Countries had their boundaries redrawn, alliances were reorganized, and established powers were forced to come to terms with new realities.

Standing in the middle of the reconstructed city was Anatoly, who had worked his way up through the ranks of the Ukrainian armed forces. Even though he was surrounded by indications that life was getting back to normal, the memories of the past continued to reverberate inside of him. The memories of the conflict were seared deeply into his heart, serving as a gloomy reminder of the price that had to be paid for their hard-won success.

Michael decided to leave the realm of intelligence and become a writer in Washington, District of Columbia. His book, which provided a riveting account of the fight from the point of view of individuals who were on the ground, was an instant hit when it was published. It was more than simply a narrative; rather, it was a demonstration of the strength of the human spirit despite the challenges that it faced.

In Moscow, General Volkov had decided to lead a retiring life of peace and quiet. The jaded veteran sought refuge in his own company, where he could think about the choices he had to make and the part he had played in determining the course of events for his nation. Even though the war had clearly left its mark on him, as seen by the lines that had begun to appear on his face, the resolve that could be seen in his eyes had not wavered.

Misha was revered across Belarus as a national hero at this point. His courageous actions had reversed the course of the battle, motivating his countrymen and countrywomen to be resilient in the face of hardship. He had made his stamp on history, becoming a symbol of defiance and tenacity in the bleakest of times, a light of hope in the face of adversity.

However, despite the fact that the globe was making progress, the conflict continued to cast a long and significant shadow. It was a spooky reminder of the price that must be paid for ambition, the precarious nature of peace, and the indomitable spirit of the human race. It was a testimony to the brave individuals who triumphed in the face of hardship, so ensuring that their names will be engraved indelibly into the annals of history.

The battle was over for Anatoly, Michael, General Volkov, and Misha, but its effect continued to be felt in their lives. It was a turning moment in their lives that had irreparably altered them, a chapter in their lives that had changed the course of their destinies. They had acted out their parts in the vast stage that was history, the threads of their narratives woven into the very fabric of time.

The sun began to set, laying long shadows across the landscapes that had been recreated, and the echoes of the past were a heartbreaking reminder of the past. They served as constant reminders of the wars that had been fought, the lives that had been sacrificed, and the triumphs that had been gained. They served as constant reminders of the iron barrier that previously partitioned the globe and of the vengeance that eventually brought about its unification.

In the end, they were reminders of the tenacious spirit of mankind, a spirit that battled for what was right, endured in the face of hardship, and dared to dream of a better tomorrow. Even in the midst of conflict, the human spirit shined brilliantly, serving as a ray of light in the midst of the stormiest of conditions.

As our narrative draws to a close, we are left with a simple yet deep truth: that even in the face of the greatest hardship, the human spirit is unbroken, rising from the ashes to carve a new path, to build a better world. This is the message that we are left with as our story comes to an end.

And at the end of the day, isn't that what it all boils down to?

ABOUT THE AUTHOR

Robert Dobbs is an accomplished author, US Army Airborne veteran, and dedicated public servant with a rich background in international relations, management consulting, and education. His life experiences and academic achievements have informed his writing, which focuses on themes of resilience, leadership, and the power of personal growth.

Born and raised in Wisconsin in the United States, Robert's military career began when he enlisted in the US Army Airborne. During his service, he was deployed to several overseas locations, where he developed a strong sense of discipline and camaraderie. After completing his military duties, he transitioned into civilian life, eager to continue serving his community in other ways.

With a passion for public service, Robert spent a decade in local elected office, where he tackled various issues related to governance, social welfare, and economic development. At the same time, he was appointed to serve on a board for the Supreme Court of Wisconsin, further showcasing his dedication to the betterment of society.

Robert's keen interest in international affairs led him to spend ten years working in the Middle East and Central Asia as an education and management consultant. Here, he played an essential role in fostering understanding and cooperation between diverse cultures and organizations.

With a Master's degree in International Relations, an MBA, and a Bachelor of Science in Public Administration, Robert's education has provided him with a solid foundation for his work in both the public and private sectors. His unique combination of military, political, and international experience has given him a distinctive voice as an author, offering readers a fresh perspective on global issues and the human experience.

In his personal life, Robert is a devoted husband and father.

www.ingramcontent.com/pod-product-compliance
Lightning Source LLC
Chambersburg PA
CBHW061627250726
48659CB00004B/1117